THE LITTLE BOOK
OF SHOCKING
FOOD FACTS

© 2010 Fiell Publishing Limited
www.fiell.com

A catalogue record for this book
is available from the British Library.

ISBN 978-1-906863-05-0

Project Concept: Charlotte & Peter Fiell
Project Management: Charlotte Fiell
Editorial: Dale Petersen
Design: Craig Holden Feinberg

Printed in China

Note: The publisher has endeavored to ensure that the information contained in this
book was correct at the time of going to press. The information in this book, however, is
not intended to replace the advice of a doctor. It is always advisable to consult a medical
practitioner before embarking on any new dietary regimes or lifestyle changes.

THE LITTLE BOOK
OF SHOCKING
FOOD FACTS

CRAIG HOLDEN FEINBERG & DALE PETERSEN

FIELL PUBLISHING LIMITED

INTRODUCTION
Dale Petersen

Food – it used to be so simple. At its most basic,
we just needed it to stay alive. But, as our technologies
and societies evolved, so too did the role of food.
Beyond sustenance, it became a source of comfort
and pleasure, and around it grew cultures and customs.
Social bonds of hospitality and feasting helped to
define communities.

    While once relatively straightforward, the realm
of food has now become increasingly problematic.
Once upon a time, meals were prepared with patience
and care from whole, healthy ingredients. Now, we
need not look far to find a microwaveable meal that
can fit in our car's cup-holder. Rather than lingering
over the dinner table, more and more meals are eaten
outside the home.

Moreover, this pales in comparison with the challenges faced by a world in which one and a half billion overfed, overweight people co-exist with nearly another billion who remain underfed or starving. Even more bizarre is the contemporary human paradox that the same person can be both obese and malnourished.

Our food choices can now bring us vitality or disease. Choose right and you get health and longevity; choose wrong and the penalty can be chronic disease and/or premature death. The scourges of modern living – heart disease, diabetes, hypertension and cancer – are held to be largely diet-related. Findings such as these place poor diet at the root of a health emergency.

We are led to believe that our inherited knowledge and concerns about food are mistaken, and that self-appointed food experts will show us a better way. Powerful lobbies work to convince us that our anxieties about pesticides, antibiotics and additives are groundless, or that the links we perceive between obesity, fast food and sugar consumption are merely coincidental. We are lulled into thinking that dinner from a box, freezer or restaurant is an acceptable lifestyle for a family concerned about nutrition.

The further we move along this evolutionary food continuum, the more we lose sight of where our food comes from. Who is growing it? How was it grown? How does it get to us? What is in it? Is it safe? All we see is a package and a price tag.

The reality is that we should be far more aware of what is going on behind the packaging: we are facing nothing less than a global food crisis, and we all need to make a stand. The fact that we are only beginning to confront these problems means that their gravity is still hard to grasp. We have been taking our food for granted, and there are controlling interests that would prefer us to remain as ignorant as possible.

The story of this crisis spans continents and oceans, and it starts with the concept of food security, defined by the UN Food and Agriculture Organization as follows:

> Food security exists when all people, at all times, have physical, social and economic access to sufficient, safe and nutritious food that meets their dietary needs and food preferences for an active and healthy life.

Food security is one of the most pressing issues facing humanity. At first glance, it would seem that this goal will have been achieved once the poorest of the poor are being fed. However, this risks oversimplifying the problem, and we should consider whether the UN's definition of security is, in fact, rather narrow. Indeed, a range of issues that impact on the global availability of food are only hinted at in the UN's description.

The first of these is sustainability: the idea that the food supplied today will still be supplied tomorrow. Security in this respect is illusory, and our decisions and actions here and now will determine whether we achieve it in the future.

Next, we should consider the financial costs of food, and not just as individual consumers, but as nations. Even a cursory analysis makes it clear that what we pay for our meals, and what they actually cost are two very different things – the price tag for communities and for the environment is often a great deal higher.

Apportioning responsibility for these costs is no easy task: the plundering of our oceans and the blighting of land through agricultural pollutants so often occurs without reparation, financial or otherwise. Similarly the congestion and harmful emissions caused by the food-transporting trucks that clog our roads are frequently ignored by business and government alike. Beyond this, there is the ethical question of who should bear the health costs of food-related medical conditions, diseases and obesity. They may not have been quantified in hard currency, but these bills are accumulating day by day. If the cost of our food was proportionate to these expenses, we might well choose very differently – and some would say that we should.

Threats to our food supply are growing in ways we could not have predicted. Small farmers, for example, are being compelled to leave their livelihoods because they can no longer feed their families, or ours. The food industry is simply failing to pay them an adequate income for their crops or livestock, and security of food supply will continue to elude us until these disadvantaged farmers have achieved some measure of equity in their dealings with the market. Food supply is also threatened by climate change and harvest failure – one natural disaster can, and often does, wipe out a complete crop cycle.

Additionally, concerns about nutrition and food safety cannot be restricted to the developing world. Affluent nations are also facing severe challenges in ensuring that dietary staples will not damage public health in the short or long term.

The scope of the unfolding crisis can be found in these varied dimensions of food security. However, the sense of urgency that they should generate is counterbalanced by the extraordinary fact that there has never been more food available per person than there is today. An achievement worth celebrating, for sure, but then why are almost a billion people starving? Who is making the decisions relating to crop selection, transportation and market economics that cause such terrible human suffering?

Well, to begin with, food corporations dictate to farmers what they should grow, and how much (or how little) they will be paid for it. They also operate vast networks for transporting and distributing farmers' produce. Supermarkets then step in and decide what we will be able to buy in their stores, and whether it will have been sourced from local markets or flown thousands of miles from another continent. The appearance of plenty disguises the reality that our power to select is very limited.

Those who dictate our food 'choices' do not necessarily share our concerns. They are not plagued by the amount of pesticides we ingest. Nor are they troubled by the amount or type of additives that go into our food, or the health risks that might be associated with them.

The market commonly assumes that consumers are only interested in keeping the cost of food down. Crucially, though, we have never been given the whole picture. If we understood that a few pence more for free range eggs would alleviate a lifetime of suffering for the laying hens, then one would hope most of us would not begrudge the extra cost. Keeping customers in ignorance of these wider issues, while ramming home the message of cheap supermarket prices, has fuelled spiralling profit margins. Supermarket executives can even cite the apathy of their own shoppers – an apathy they have carefully nurtured – as the justification for leaving their business practices unreformed.

There is plenty here to shock us all. Those with environmental interests may be taken aback by the extent of these unsustainable practices. Those with concerns about health may be appalled by the decline in our food's nutritional value. None of us can, in conscience, be anything other than outraged at the extent of starvation and malnutrition in our world of plenty.

In a more positive sense, what is also remarkable is the degree of control we can exert over our health by making good nutritional decisions. We have never possessed such power to reduce or eliminate the impact of chronic diseases on ourselves, our families and our communities. Good health is not just the random gift of fate or genetic inheritance: we have a significant amount of control over our vulnerability to cancer, Alzheimer's, or even hypertension. The empowering reality is that vitality can be in our hands.

This is the story of the state of our food, told one image and one fact at a time. Its intention is to provide an informed and accessible guide to the issues that lie behind the food we eat today, concerns that are both close to home and global. You may use what follows to make some positive changes to your relationship with food. You might, for instance, decide to keep your food spending closer to home, or insist on goods produced in an ethical fashion. You might choose to purchase food that has been sustainably managed. Individually, these might seem to be trivial statements, but once they are embraced collectively their impact will multiply changing food production and consumption for good. Maybe, together,

we can right some of the wrongs that currently endanger our food system.

We do not need to be doing all the damage that we are. We can feed the hungry. We can make healthful food choices. But, first we have to inform ourselves, and with that knowledge comes the power to bring about change.

Already small revolutions are happening, and the pendulum is starting to swing back. Grass roots movements are springing up, determined to bring ethical values back into our food; restaurants are sourcing locally, and the sustainability of fish stocks is gaining the attention it deserves. Sales of organic food are growing by leaps and bounds, and people are consciously making the effort to buy more of their produce directly from farmers' markets. Around the world, farmers are joining together to improve production methods and working conditions, and to boost their incomes.

The time is right for a food epiphany, and here it is: good health comes from good food, grown in a responsible manner and made available to everyone. This should not be too much for us to ask for.

Do not underestimate the power of the vote you cast every time you buy something to eat. Every day you really can vote for change, over and over again.

And as a last bit of inspiration, consider the words of a woman once called "Mother of the World" by *Time* magazine, the great anthropologist Margaret Meade:

NEVER DOUBT THAT A SMALL GROUP OF THOUGHTFUL, COMMITTED CITIZENS CAN CHANGE THE WORLD. INDEED, IT IS THE ONLY THING THAT EVER HAS.

THERE ARE CURRENTLY 923 MILLION STARVING PEOPLE IN THE WORLD.

FOOD AND AGRICULTURE ORGANIZATION OF THE UNITED NATIONS (FAO), 2008

CHINESE MEAT CONSUMPTION PER PERSON HAS MORE THAN DOUBLED SINCE 1995, FROM 25 KG (55 LB) PER PERSON TO 53 KG (117 LB).

BIOFUELS DIGEST, 2008

GLOBAL FOOD PRICES HAVE RISEN BY 130% SINCE 2002, AND BIOFUEL PRODUCTION IS RESPONSIBLE FOR 75% OF THAT INCREASE.

THE WORLD BANK, DEVELOPMENT PROSPECTS GROUP, 2008

TWO-THIRDS OF AMERICANS ARE OVERWEIGHT OR OBESE.

NATIONAL CENTER FOR HEALTH STATISTICS, 2006

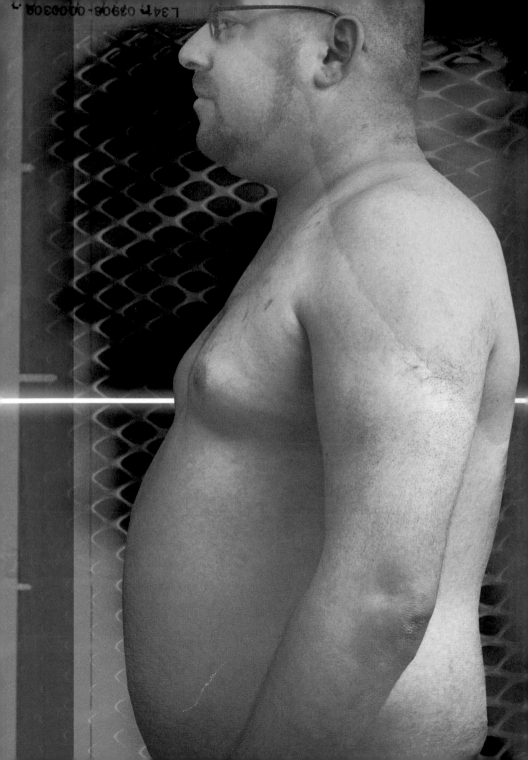

FREE

MORE THAN HALF OF SUPERMARKET MULTI-BUY PROMOTIONS ARE FOR HIGH-FAT OR HIGH-SUGAR FOODS, DESPITE THE FACT THAT HEALTH ADVICE DICTATES THESE SHOULD NOT MAKE UP MORE THAN 7% OF OUR DIET.

NATIONAL CONSUMER COUNCIL, 2008

MORE THAN IO MILLION CHILDREN DIE EVERY YEAR AND THE UNDERLYING CAUSE FOR MOST OF THESE DEATHS IS STARVATION.

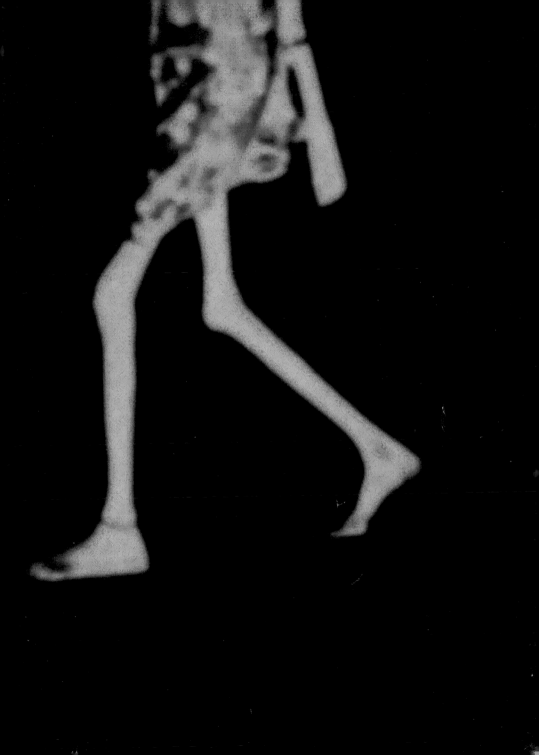

LETTUCE HAS BEEN KNOWN TO RECEIVE 4 SPRAY ROUNDS OF INSECTICIDES, 2 SPRAY ROUNDS OF FUNGICIDES, AND 2 SPRAY ROUNDS OF HERBICIDES DURING ITS GROWTH CYCLE.

DEPARTMENT FOR ENVIRONMENT, FOOD AND RURAL AFFAIRS (DEFRA) & SCOTTISH EXECUTIVE ENVIRONMENT AND RURAL AFFAIRS DEPARTMENT, 1999

IN THE UNITED STATES MORE
THAN 3,000 PEOPLE DIE EACH
YEAR AS A RESULT OF CHOKING,
MAINLY ON FOOD.

THE AMERICAN RED CROSS, 2009

VITAMIN A DEFICIENCY WILL CAUSE UP TO 500,000 CHILDREN TO GO BLIND EVERY YEAR; HALF OF THEM WILL DIE WITHIN A YEAR OF LOSING THEIR SIGHT.

WORLD HEALTH ORGANIZATION, 2007

MOST PEOPLE DRINK ABOUT 2 LITRES OF WATER A DAY, BUT CONSUME 3,000 LITRES A DAY IF THE WATER THAT GOES INTO PRODUCING THEIR FOOD IS TAKEN INTO ACCOUNT.

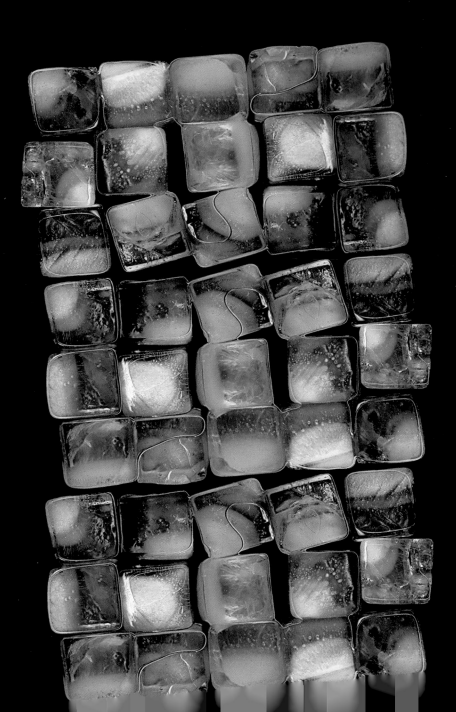

IN THE UNITED STATES LIVESTOCK CONSUMES MORE THAN 7 TIMES AS MUCH GRAIN AS IS CONSUMED DIRECTLY BY THE COUNTRY'S ENTIRE HUMAN POPULATION.

AMERICAN JOURNAL OF CLINICAL NUTRITION, 2003

ONE IN THREE AFRICANS ARE MALNOURISHED AND ABOUT HALF OF THE CONTINENT'S NEARLY 700 MILLION PEOPLE LIVE ON LESS THAN $1 A DAY.

BREAD FOR THE WORLD INSTITUTE, 2003

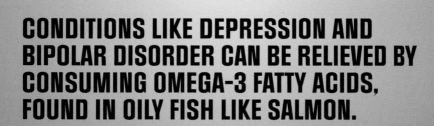

CONDITIONS LIKE DEPRESSION AND BIPOLAR DISORDER CAN BE RELIEVED BY CONSUMING OMEGA-3 FATTY ACIDS, FOUND IN OILY FISH LIKE SALMON.

JOURNAL OF CLINICAL PSYCHIATRY, 2006

BASED ON CURRENT TRENDS, THE GLOBAL FISHING INDUSTRY WILL BE IN A STATE OF COMPLETE COLLAPSE BY 2048.

SCIENCE, 2006

THE ANTIOXIDANTS THAT ARE ABUNDANT IN FRUITS, VEGETABLES AND TEA ARE VALUABLE TO US BECAUSE THEY PROVIDE A LONGER LIFE, REDUCED CANCER RISK, AND LOWER THE INCIDENCE OF CARDIO-VASCULAR DISEASE.

BRITISH FOOD JOURNAL, 1995

YOU CAN PROTECT AGAINST AGE-RELATED MACULAR DEGENERATION BY EATING FOODS HIGH IN LUTEIN AND ZEAXANTHIN SUCH AS CORN, PEPPERS, EGGS, KIWI FRUIT, GRAPES, AND ZUCCHINI (COURGETTE).

BRITISH JOURNAL OF OPHTHALMOLOGY, 1998

TOMATOES, ESPECIALLY COOKED TOMATOES, CAN PROTECT AGAINST PROSTATE CANCER.

CANCER RESEARCH, 1999

FOOD COLOURINGS AND ADDITIVES INCREASE HYPERACTIVITY IN CHILDREN.

THE LANCET, 2007

EVERY YEAR IN THE UNITED STATES,
UP TO 25 MILLION POUNDS (11.3 MILLION KG)
OF ANTIMICROBIAL DRUGS (ANTIBIOTICS,
ANTIVIRALS, ANTIFUNGALS AND ANTI-
PARASITICS) ARE FED TO LIVESTOCK FOR
NON-THERAPEUTIC PURPOSES.

UNION OF CONCERNED SCIENTISTS, 2001

The Deluxe **LOOK WHAT'S NEW** PILL CASE POWER 2000

*This product is not child proof.

By **Cowtrex**®

WE TAKE PRIDE IN MANAGING YOUR CATTLE'S MEDICATION.

Moo!!!

1-800-COW-TREX
269-8739

24-Hour Operator Assistance
Order now!

DRIVE
THRU

EATING AT FAST FOOD RESTAURANTS TWO OR MORE TIMES A WEEK IS STRONGLY ASSOCIATED WITH WEIGHT GAIN AND INSULIN RESISTANCE, LEADING TO AN INCREASED RISK OF OBESITY AND TYPE 2 DIABETES.

HAMBURGER BASKETS

HAMBURGER	$5.60
CHEESEBURGER	$6.50
JUMBO HAMBURGER	$6.50
JUMBO CHEESEBURGER	$6.95
BACON HAMBURGER	$6.25
BACON CHEESEBURGER	$6.75
CHILI BURGER	$6.50
MUSHROOM SWISS	$6.75
BAILEY DOG	$4.95
▶ *ADD ONION RINGS TO ANY BASKET*	$0.80

All burgers served with lettuce, tomato, onion, pickles, and mustard

HAMBURGER

HAMBURGER	$4.50
CHEESEBURGER	$4.75
JUMBO HAMBURGER	$5.50
JUMBO CHEESEBURGER	$5.95
BACON HAMBURGER	$5.00
BACON CHEESEBURGER	$5.75
CHILI BURGER	$6.50
MUSHROOM SWISS	$5.50
BAILEY DOG	$3.75
▶ *ADD BACON TO ANY BURGER*	$0.80

SIDE ORDERS

SIDE SALAD	$1.50
FRENCH FRIES	$2.50
ONION RINGS	$2.95

SANDWICHES

CHICKEN FRIED STEAK	$4.50
HAM & CHEESE CLUB	$4.75
TURKEY CLUB	$5.50
B.L.T	$5.95
GRILLED CHICKEN	$5.00
GRILLED HAM & CHEESE	$5.75
GRILLED CHEESE & FRENCH FRIES	$6.50
MUSHROOM SWISS	$5.50
BAILEY DOG	$3.75
▶ *ADD ONION RINGS TO ANY BASKET*	$0.80

DINNERS

CHICKEN FRIED CHICKEN	$7.45
CHICKEN FRIED STEAK	$7.50
GRILLED CHICKEN DINNER	$7.00
HAMBURGER STEAK	$7.95
JUMBO SHRIMP PLATTER	$7.25
OPEN FISH PLATTER	$7.75
FISHERMAN'S FEAST PLATTER	$10.50
CHICKEN TENDERS	$6.50
GRILLED CHICKEN SALAD	$6.25
CHEF SALAD	$6.25

CHILDREN'S MENU

CHEESEBURGER–HOT DOG–CHICKEN TENDERS–GRILLED CHEESE
Served with french fries and drink $3.75, extra trimming add $0.50

DRINKS & DESSERTS

SODA	$1.40
COFFEE	$7.50
ROOT BEER FLOAT	$3.00
MALTS & SHAKES	$2.95
SUNDAE	$3.25
BANANA SPLIT	$4.25

AMERICANS SPEND 49% OF THEIR FOOD DOLLARS AWAY FROM HOME.

UNITED STATES DEPARTMENT OF AGRICULTURE, 2008

"ALL YOU CAN EAT" CATFISH $10.50 WED. & FRI. 5PM-8PM

TUESDAY – FRIDAY – 7:00AM-10:00PM
SUNDAY 8:00AM FOR BREAKFAST & LUNCH
SATURDAY 8:00AM-9:00PM

AMERICANS SPEND $55 BILLION PER YEAR ON WEIGHT LOSS PRODUCTS AND SERVICES.

U.S. WEIGHT LOSS & DIET CONTROL MARKET (9TH EDITION), MARKETDATA ENTERPRISES, INC., 2007

IN THE DEVELOPED WORLD, PEOPLE CONSUME ABOUT 4.5 KG (10 LB) OF FOOD ADDITIVES PER YEAR, JUMPING TO 11.5 KG (25 LB) IF YOU INCLUDE THEIR SALT INTAKE.

CONCISE ENCYCLOPEDIA OF FOODS & NUTRITION, CRC PRESS, 1994

27% OR 96 BILLION POUNDS (43 BILLION KG) OF AVAILABLE FOOD IS WASTED IN THE U.S. EACH YEAR.

ECONOMIC RESEARCH SERVICE, USDA, 1997

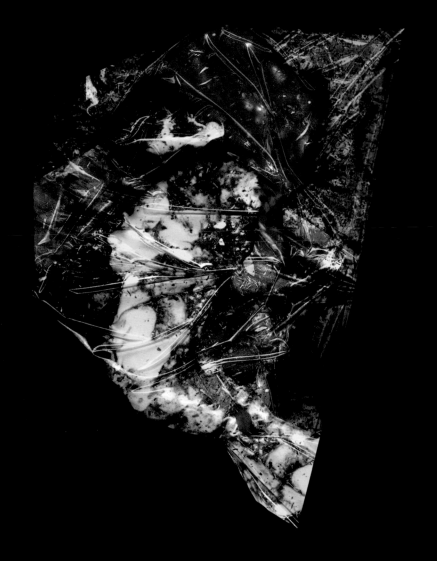

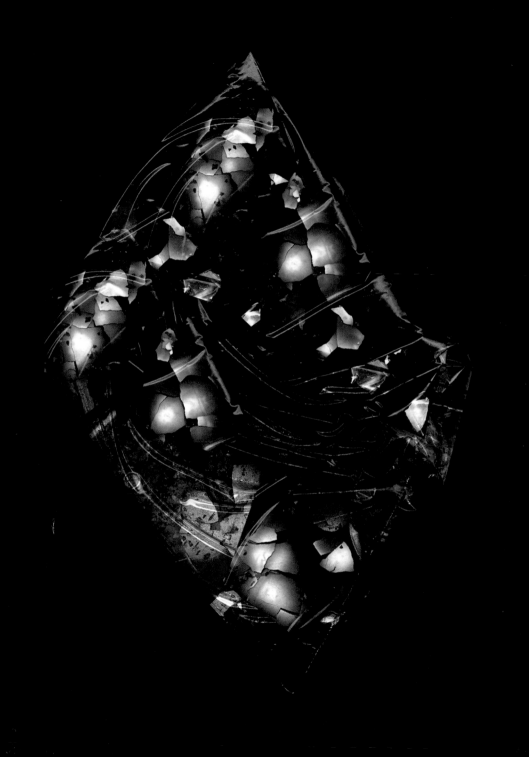

EACH YEAR IN THE U.S. FOODBORNE DISEASES RESULT IN 76 MILLION ILLNESSES, 325,000 HOSPITALISATIONS AND 5,000 DEATHS.

CENTERS FOR DISEASE CONTROL AND PREVENTION, 1999

DROUGHT CURRENTLY RANKS AS THE SINGLE MOST COMMON CAUSE OF FOOD SHORTAGES.

FOOD AND AGRICULTURE ORGANIZATION OF THE UNITED NATIONS, 2003

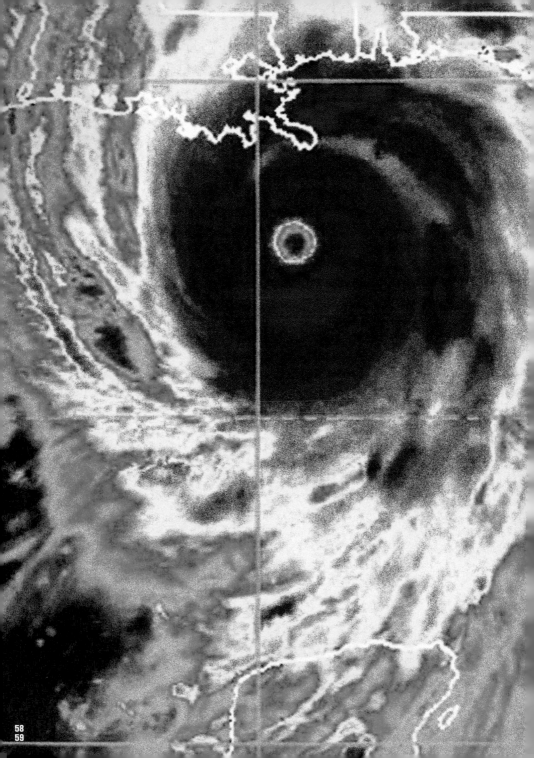

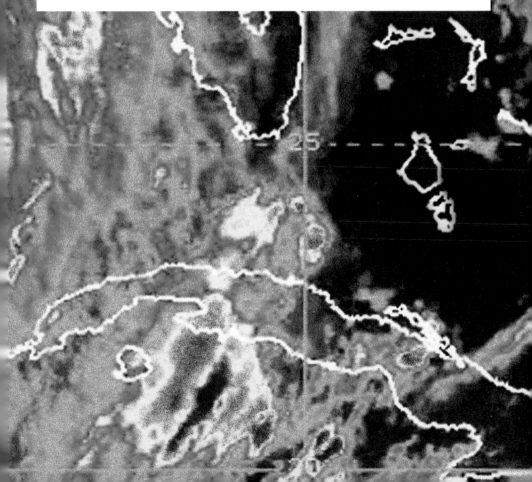

NATURAL DISASTERS, SUCH AS FLOODS AND CYCLONES, ARE NOW HAPPENING AT A RATE OF 400-500 PER YEAR, AN INCREASE FROM 125 IN THE EARLY 1980s, CAUSING UNTOLD DEVASTATION AS THEY WIPE OUT CROPS AND ADD TO THE SEVERE GLOBAL HUNGER SITUATION.

UNITED NATIONS INTERNATIONAL STRATEGY FOR DISASTER REDUCTION
SECRETARIAT (UNISDR), 2007

IN LESS THAN 20 YEARS THE PROPORTION OF FOOD CRISES CAUSED BY HUMANS HAS MORE THAN DOUBLED, INCREASING FROM 15% TO OVER 35%, WITH MANY OF THESE EMERGENCIES TRIGGERED BY CONFLICT.

WORLD FOOD PROGRAMME, 2008

THE AGRIBUSINESS SECTOR SPENT IN EXCESS OF $139 MILLION LOBBYING THE U.S. GOVERNMENT IN 2008.

THE CENTER FOR RESPONSIVE POLITICS, 2009

THE AGRICULTURE INDUSTRY USES 1,200 MILLION LB (545 MILLION KG) OF PESTICIDES OVER THE COURSE OF A YEAR IN THE U.S. ALONE.

U.S. ENVIRONMENTAL PROTECTION AGENCY, 2004

A REDUCTION IN THE MINERAL CONTENT OF FRUITS AND VEGETABLES HAS BEEN SEEN OVER TIME IN THE U.K., WITH DECLINES OF UP TO 80%.

BRITISH FOOD JOURNAL, 1997

BREAST-FED INFANTS HAVE LOWER RATES OF HOSPITAL ADMISSIONS, EAR INFECTIONS, DIARRHOEA, RASHES, ALLERGIES, AND OTHER MEDICAL PROBLEMS THAN BOTTLE-FED BABIES.

U.S. FOOD AND DRUG ADMINISTRATION, 1995 & 1996

PHTHALATES ARE CHEMICALS, USED IN CONSUMER PRODUCTS AND FOOD PACKAGING, WHICH FIND THEIR WAY INTO FOODS SUCH AS INFANT FORMULA AND BABY FOOD AND ARE KNOWN TO DISRUPT REPRODUCTIVE DEVELOPMENT.

TOXICOLOGICAL SCIENCES, 2000

27 MILLION TONS OF FISH ARE DISCARDED AS WASTE EVERY YEAR.

FOOD AND AGRICULTURE ORGANIZATION OF THE UNITED NATIONS, 1994

IN TROPICAL AREAS, THE BYCATCH-TO-SHRIMP RATIO CAN BE ROUGHLY 10:1.

WORLDWATCH INSTITUTE, 2004

EXCITOTOXINS CAUSE THE NEURONS IN OUR BRAIN TO EXCITE THEMSELVES TO DEATH. THEY ARE A GROUP OF CHEMICALS AND FOOD ADDITIVES SUCH AS ASPARTAME AND MSG, AND ARE COMMONLY FOUND IN OUR FOOD AND DRINKS.

RUSSELL L. BLAYLOCK M.D. EXCITOTOXINS: THE TASTE THAT KILLS, HEALTH PRESS, 1996

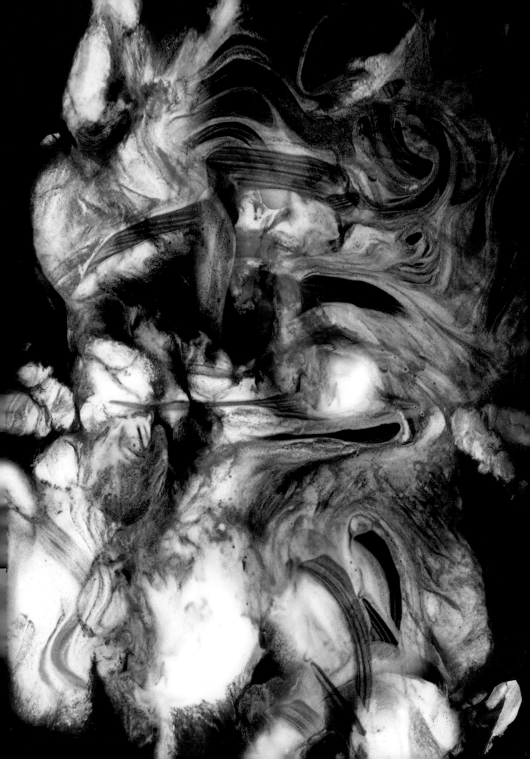

EATING APPLES AND ONIONS
CAN IMPROVE THE INFLAMMATION
ASSOCIATED WITH CONDITIONS
LIKE RHEUMATOID ARTHRITIS.

FARMACO, 2001

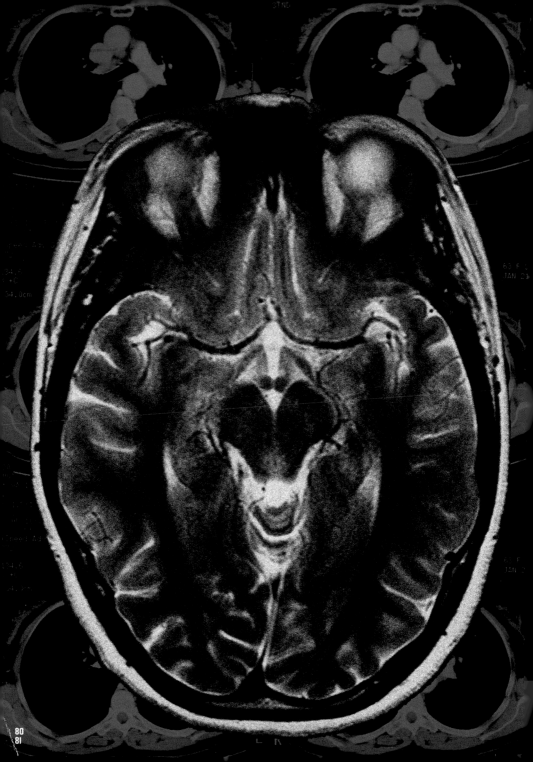

BLUEBERRIES CAN PROTECT YOUR BRAIN FROM THE EFFECTS OF AGING.

NEUROBIOLOGY OF AGING, 2005

THE RATE OF OBESITY AMONGST MEN IN ENGLAND HAS INCREASED BY 75% SINCE I993.

NATIONAL HEALTH SERVICE, 2006

ABOUT 280,000 AMERICANS DIE EVERY YEAR AS A DIRECT RESULT OF BEING OVERWEIGHT.

JOURNAL OF THE AMERICAN MEDICAL ASSOCIATION, 1999

GLOBALLY, EACH YEAR MORE THAN 56 BILLION ANIMALS ARE RAISED AS LIVESTOCK FOR SLAUGHTER.

FOOD AND AGRICULTURE ORGANIZATION OF THE UNITED NATIONS, 2008

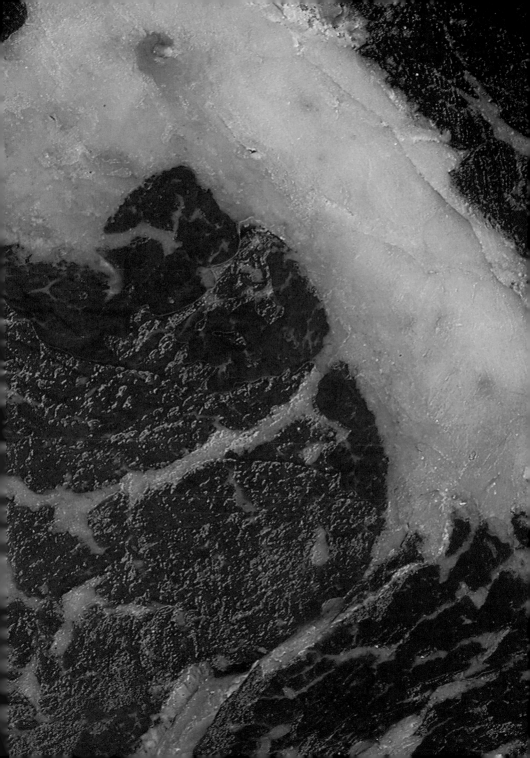

INSTRUCTIONS
FROM INSPECTED AND PASSED
FOOD PRODUCTS MAY CONTAIN
ILLNESS IF THE PRODUCT IS MIS-
ERLY FOR YOUR PROTECTION,
INSTRUCTIONS.

D OR FROZEN.
ATOR OR MICROWAVE.

ID POULTRY SEPARATE FROM OTHER
KING SURFACES (INCLUDING CUTTING
S AND HANDS AFTER TOUCHING RAW
Y.

LY.

HOT. REFRIGERATE LEFTOVERS
DISCARD.

IT TAKES 100,000 LITRES OF WATER TO PRODUCE 1 KG OF BEEF.

**DAVID & MARCIA PIMENTEL, FOOD, ENERGY AND
SOCIETY, COLORADO UNIVERSITY PRESS, 1996**

INSTRUCTIONS
FROM INSPECTED AND PASSED
FOOD PRODUCTS MAY CONTAIN
ILLNESS IF THE PRODUCT IS MIS-
ERLY FOR YOUR PROTECTION,
INSTRUCTIONS.

O OR FROZEN.
ATOR OR MICROWAVE.

ID POULTRY SEPARATE FROM OTHER
KING SURFACES (INCLUDING CUTTING
S AND HANDS AFTER TOUCHING RAW
Y.

LY.

HOT. REFRIGERATE LEFTOVERS
DISCARD.

SAFE HANDLING INSTRUCTIONS
THIS PRODUCT WAS PREPARED FROM INSPECTED AND PASSED
MEAT AND/OR POULTRY. SOME FOOD PRODUCTS MAY CONTAIN
BACTERIA THAT COULD CAUSE ILLNESS IF THE PRODUCT IS MIS-
HANDLED OR COOKED IMPROPERLY. FOR YOUR PROTECTION,
FOLLOW THESE SAFE HANDLING INSTRUCTIONS.

KEEP REFRIGERATED OR FROZEN.
THAW IN REFRIGERATOR OR MICROWAVE.

KEEP RAW MEAT AND POULTRY SEPARATE FROM OTHER
FOODS. WASH WORKING SURFACES (INCLUDING CUTTING
BOARDS), UTENSILS AND HANDS AFTER TOUCHING RAW
MEAT OR POULTRY.

COOK THOROUGHLY.

KEEP HOT FOODS HOT. REFRIGERATE LEFTOVERS
IMMEDIATELY OR DISCARD.

18% OF GLOBAL GREENHOUSE GAS EMISSIONS ARE ATTRIBUTABLE TO LIVESTOCK PRODUCTION—MORE THAN THE TRANSPORTATION SECTOR.

FOOD AND AGRICULTURE ORGANIZATION OF THE UNITED NATIONS, 2006

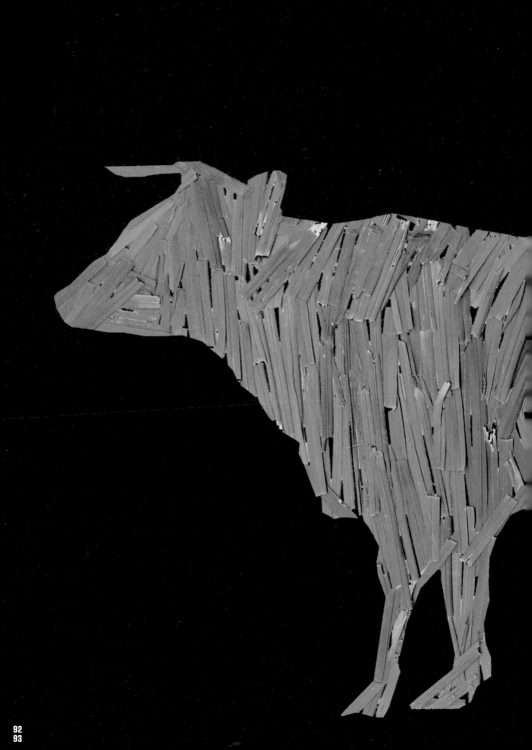

GRASS-FED, ORGANICALLY RAISED COWS PRODUCE MILK AND BEEF THAT HAVE SIGNIFICANTLY HIGHER AMOUNTS OF OMEGA-3 FATTY ACIDS, VITAMIN E, AND OTHER IMPORTANT NUTRIENTS.

FOOD CHEMISTRY, 2003

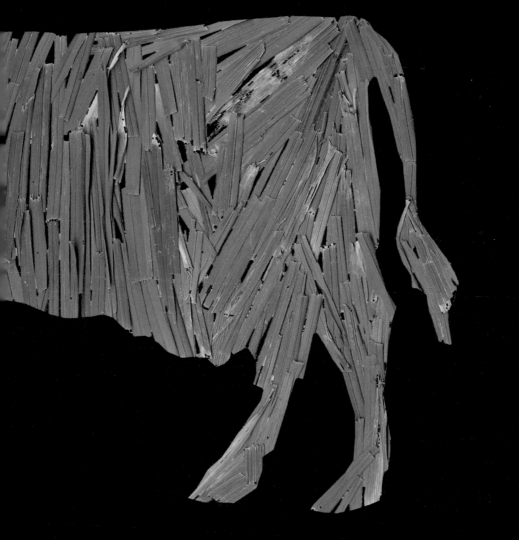

BROCCOLI, AND ITS FAMILY OF CRUCIFEROUS VEGETABLES, CONTAINS SULFORAPHANE WHICH HAS BEEN PROVEN TO INHIBIT THE GROWTH OF BREAST CANCER.

THE JOURNAL OF NUTRITION, 2004

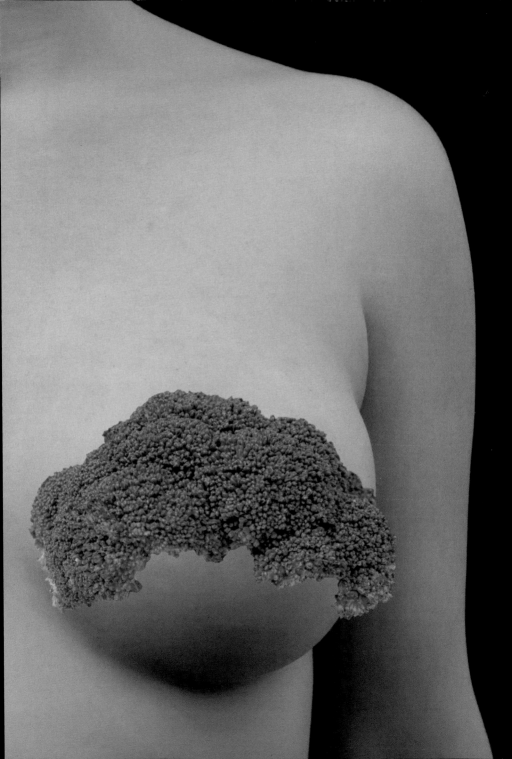

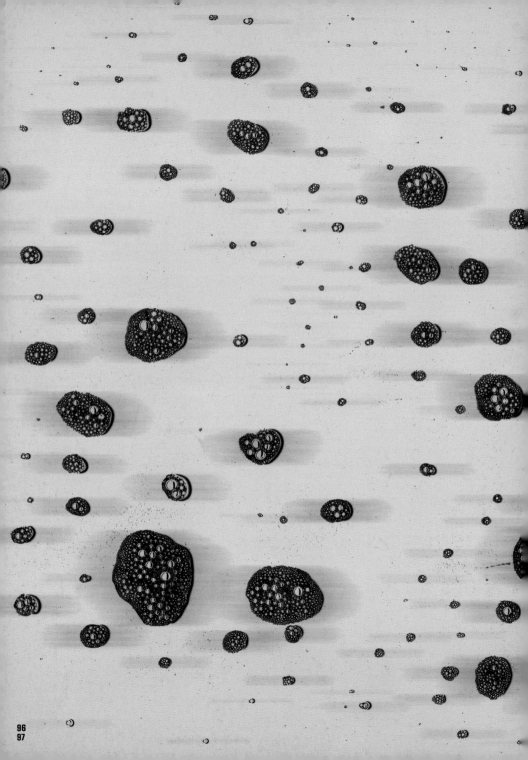

CURCUMIN, A COMPOUND IN TURMERIC AND CURRY POWDER, STOPS THE GROWTH OF CERTAIN CANCER CELLS AND PROTECTS THE BRAIN AGAINST PARKINSON'S DISEASE.

NUTRITION AND CANCER, 1996

RESVERATROL, AN INGREDIENT IN RED GRAPES, RED GRAPE JUICE AND RED WINE, HAS BEEN SHOWN TO HAVE SIGNIFICANT BENEFICIAL EFFECTS ON CHOLESTEROL LEVELS.

AMERICAN JOURNAL OF CLINICAL NUTRITION, 2006

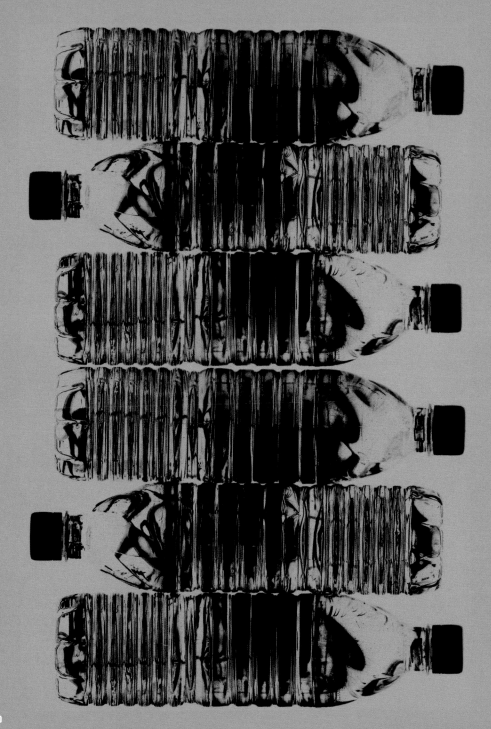

BOTTLED WATER HAS BEEN FOUND TO BE NO DIFFERENT THAN TAP WATER, CONTAINING THE SAME CONTAMINANTS BUT AT 1,900 TIMES THE PRICE.

ENVIRONMENTAL WORKING GROUP, 2008

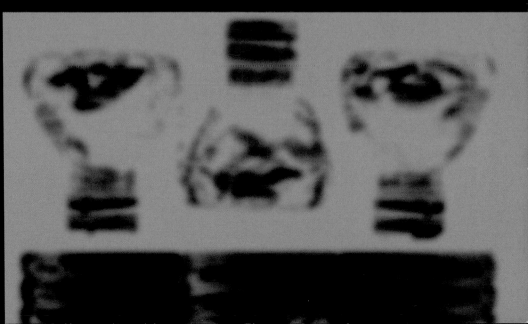

AGRICULTURE ACCOUNTS FOR MORE THAN 70% OF THE WORLD'S TOTAL WATER USE.

UN-WATER AND THE FOOD AND AGRICULTURE ORGANIZATION OF THE UNITED NATIONS, 2007

AGRICULTURE IS RESPONSIBLE FOR 70% OF THE WATER POLLUTION IN THE UNITED STATES.

OFFICE OF WASTEWATER MANAGEMENT, 1998

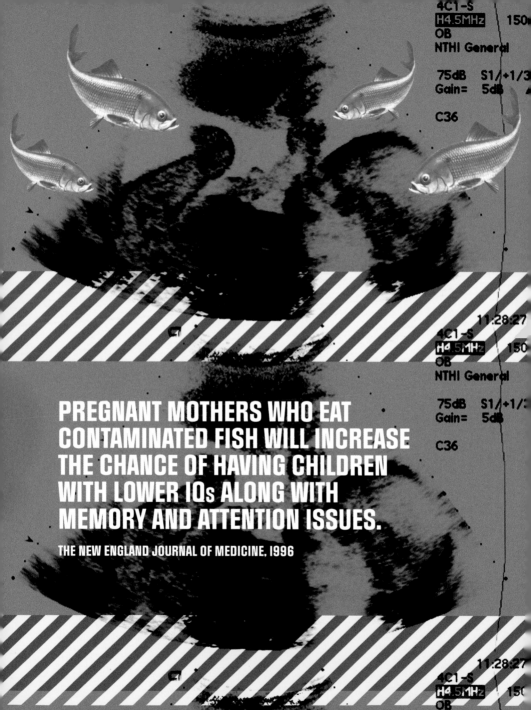

PREGNANT MOTHERS WHO EAT
CONTAMINATED FISH WILL INCREASE
THE CHANCE OF HAVING CHILDREN
WITH LOWER IQs ALONG WITH
MEMORY AND ATTENTION ISSUES.

THE NEW ENGLAND JOURNAL OF MEDICINE, 1996

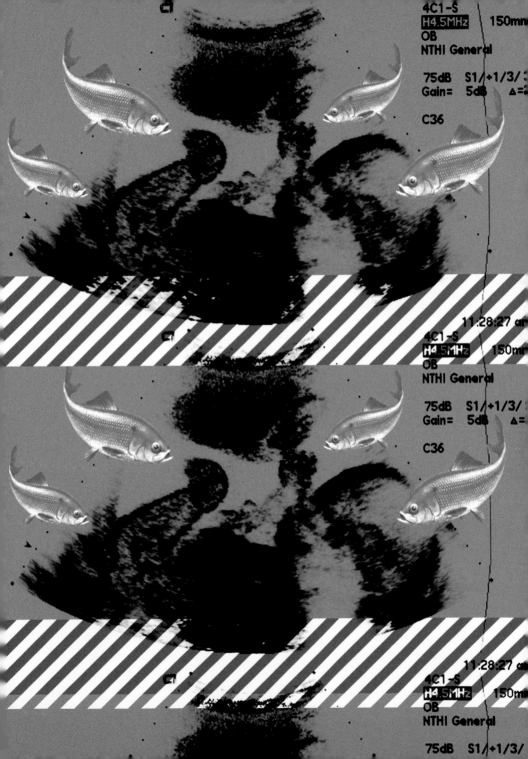

THE GULF OF MEXICO CONTAINS AN
AREA OF UP TO 20,000 KM^2 (THE SIZE
OF NEW JERSEY) REFERRED TO AS
A DEAD ZONE—SO CALLED BECAUSE
NOTHING CAN LIVE THERE DUE TO THE
OXYGEN-DEPLETION CAUSED BY
FERTILISER RUN-OFF.

JOURNAL OF ENVIRONMENTAL QUALITY, 2001

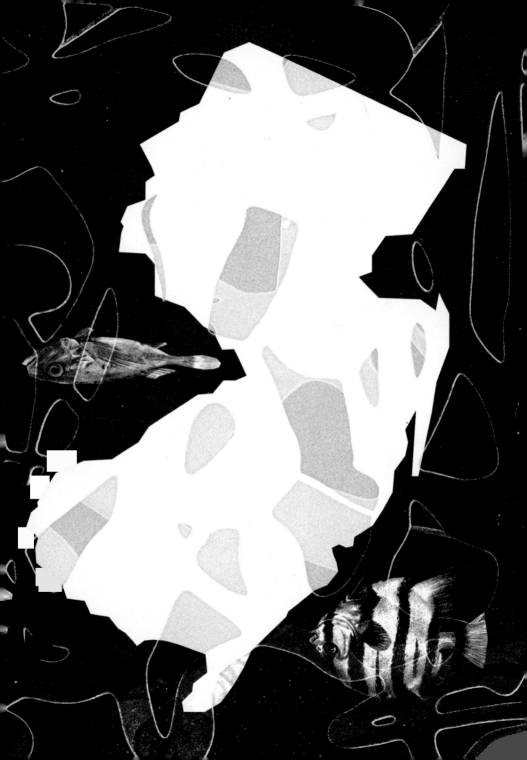

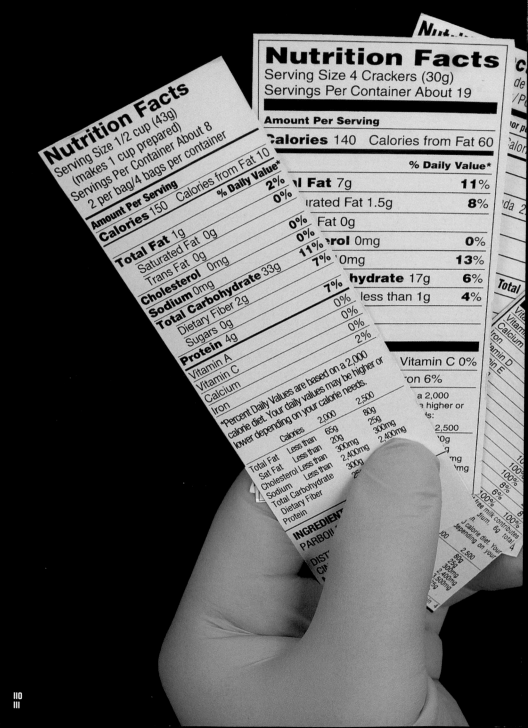

Nutrition Facts
Serving Size 1/2 cup (43g)
(makes 1 cup prepared)
Servings Per Container About 8
2 per bag/4 bags per container

Amount Per Serving

Calories 150   Calories from Fat 10

% Daily Value*

Total Fat 1g	2%
Saturated Fat 0g	0%
Trans Fat 0g	
Cholesterol 0mg	0%
Sodium 0mg	0%
Total Carbohydrate 33g	11%
Dietary Fiber 2g	7%
Sugars 0g	
Protein 4g	

Vitamin A
Vitamin C
Calcium
Iron

*Percent Daily Values are based on a 2,000
calorie diet. Your daily values may be higher or
lower depending on your calorie needs.

	Calories	2,000	2,500
Total Fat	Less than	65g	80g
Sat Fat	Less than	20g	25g
Cholesterol	Less than	300mg	300mg
Sodium	Less than	2,400mg	2,400mg
Total Carbohydrate		300g	
Dietary Fiber		25	
Protein			

INGREDIENT
PARBOI

DIST
CI

Nutrition Facts
Serving Size 4 Crackers (30g)
Servings Per Container About 19

Amount Per Serving

Calories 140   Calories from Fat 60

% Daily Value*

Total Fat 7g	11%
Saturated Fat 1.5g	8%
Trans Fat 0g	
Cholesterol 0mg	0%
Sodium 0mg	13%
Carbohydrate 17g	6%
less than 1g	4%

Vitamin C 0%
Iron 6%

a 2,000
higher or
s:

2,500
0g
g
mg
mg

Nutrition

Total

Vitamin
Vitamin
Calcium
Iron
Vitamin D
Vitamin E

94% OF SURVEY RESPONDENTS IN THE U.K. FEEL THAT ALL FOOD CONTAINING GENETICALLY MODIFIED MATERIAL SHOULD BE LABELLED.

CENTRE FOR ENVIRONMENTAL RISK, 2004

MICE FED GENETICALLY MODIFIED FOOD EXPERIENCED SIGNIFICANTLY REDUCED FERTILITY.

AUSTRIAN AGENCY FOR HEALTH AND FOOD SAFETY (AGES), 2008

AGRICULTURAL WORKERS ARE TWICE AS LIKELY TO DIE ON THE JOB AS WORKERS IN OTHER SECTORS.

INTERNATIONAL LABOUR ORGANIZATION, 1997

CONSUMERS WORLDWIDE SPENT £1.1 BILLION ON FAIRTRADE-CERTIFIED PRODUCTS IN 2006, A 42% INCREASE FROM THE PREVIOUS YEAR, WHICH DIRECTLY BENEFITED OVER 7 MILLION PEOPLE IN DEVELOPING COUNTRIES.

THE FAIRTRADE FOUNDATION, 2007

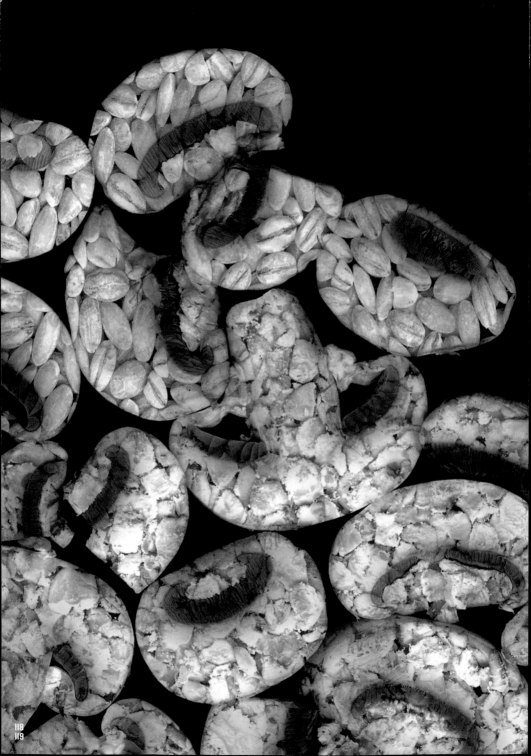

MUSHROOMS, ALONG WITH BARLEY AND OATS, CONTAIN BETA-GLUCANS, WHICH ARE ABLE TO STIMULATE THE IMMUNE SYSTEM TO OVERCOME BACTERIAL, VIRAL, FUNGAL AND PARASITIC INFECTIONS.

MUTATION RESEARCH, 2008

GREEN TEA IS A VERY EFFECTIVE CANCER INHIBITOR AND PREVENTER.

JOURNAL OF THE NATIONAL CANCER INSTITUTE, 1997

AMERICANS EAT ALMOST TRIPLE (167%)
THE AMOUNT OF RECOMMENDED SUGAR,
A SOURCE OF 500 DAILY CALORIES AND 23%
OF THE SUGGESTED CALORIC INTAKE.

USDA ECONOMIC RESEARCH SERVICE, 1999

CLOSE TO ONE QUARTER OF THE U.S. POPULATION SUFFERS FROM A CONDITION CALLED METABOLIC SYNDROME, WHICH RESULTS IN AN INABILITY TO PROCESS SUGAR.

JOURNAL OF THE AMERICAN MEDICAL ASSOCIATION, 2002

HIGH-FRUCTOSE CORN SYRUP (HFCS), THE SWEETENER USED IN MOST SOFT DRINKS AND MANY PROCESSED FOODS, IS METABOLISED DIRECTLY INTO BODY FAT.

AMERICAN JOURNAL OF CLINICAL NUTRITION, 2004

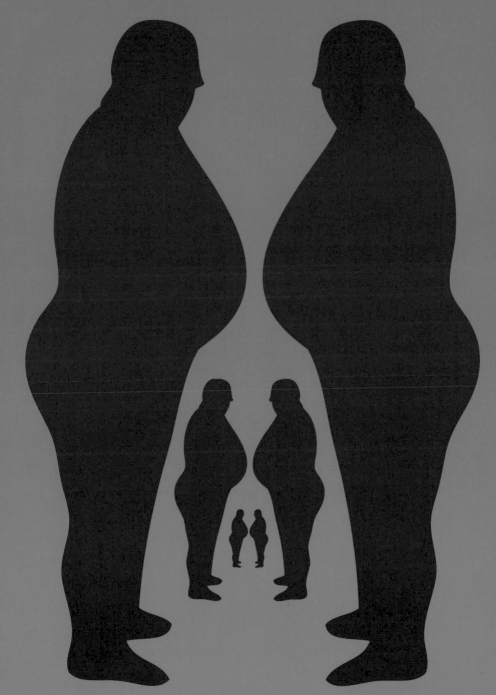

INCREASED CONSUMPTION OF SUGAR-SWEETENED DRINKS INCREASES THE LIKELIHOOD OF WEIGHT GAIN AND THE RISK OF TYPE 2 DIABETES.

JOURNAL OF THE AMERICAN MEDICAL ASSOCIATION, 2004

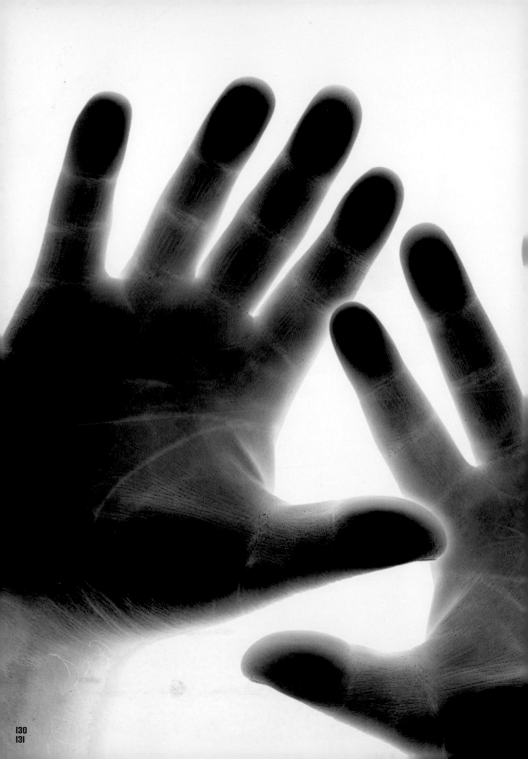

GLOBALLY, THERE ARE 3 MILLION CASES OF ACUTE PESTICIDE POISONINGS EACH YEAR, RESULTING IN 220,000 DEATHS.

WORLD HEALTH STATISTICS QUARTERLY, 1990

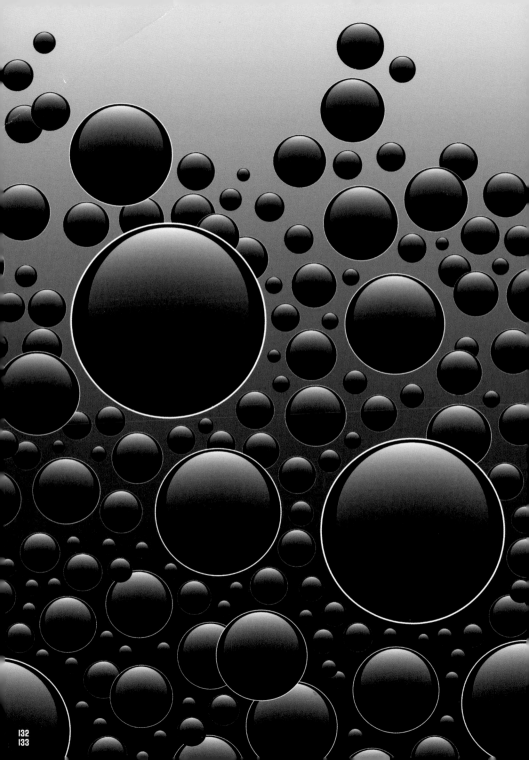

CARBONATED CAFFEINATED DRINKS LEACH CALCIUM FROM BONES THEREBY CONTRIBUTING SIGNIFICANTLY TO OSTEOPOROSIS.

AMERICAN JOURNAL OF CLINICAL NUTRITION, 2001

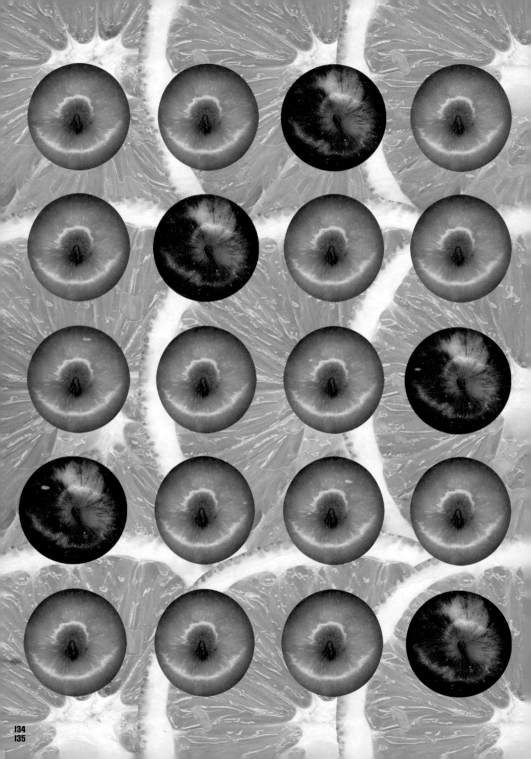

ORGANIC CROPS CONTAIN HIGHER LEVELS OF IMPORTANT NUTRIENTS THAN CONVENTIONALLY GROWN CROPS.

JOURNAL OF ALTERNATIVE AND COMPLEMENTARY MEDICINE, 2001

BENZENE, A TOXIC AND CARCINOGENIC CHEMICAL, HAS BEEN FOUND IN SOFT DRINKS AND OTHER BEVERAGES HAVING BEEN FORMED BY A MIXTURE OF THEIR INGREDIENTS.

U.S. FOOD AND DRUG ADMINISTRATION, CFSAN/OFFICE OF FOOD ADDITIVE SAFETY, 2007

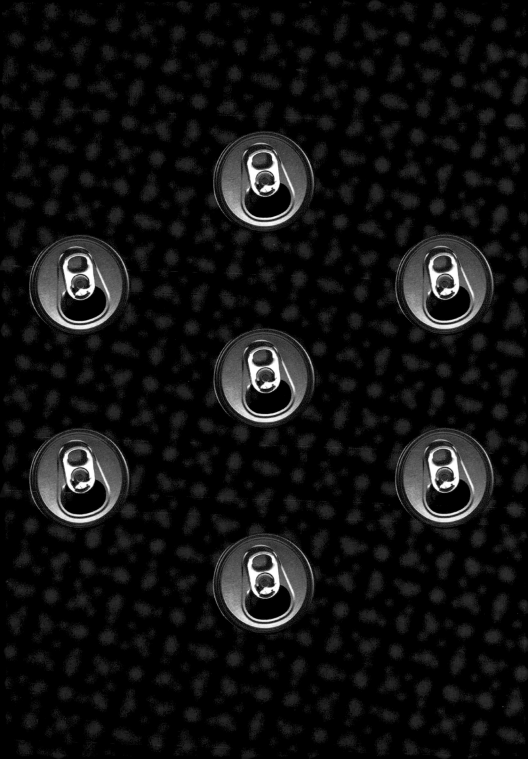

ONCE INGESTED, THE ARTIFICIAL SWEETENER ASPARTAME CONVERTS INTO FORMALDEHYDE, A TOXIC AND CARCINOGENIC SUBSTANCE, WHICH THEN ACCUMULATES IN TISSUES SUCH AS THE LIVER, KIDNEYS AND BRAIN.

LIFE SCIENCES, 1998

IN AMERICA, 63% OF SATURDAY MORNING
TV ADVERTISING, MOSTLY AIMED AT CHILDREN,
IS FOR FOOD PRODUCTS. A THIRD OF THESE
ADVERTS ARE FOR HIGH-SUGAR CEREALS,
AND THE REST FOR FOOD WITH OVERALL POOR
NUTRITIONAL VALUE.

AMERICAN JOURNAL OF HEALTH BEHAVIOR, 1999

I LB / 2.2 KG OF BODY FAT
ACTUAL SIZE

THE FINANCIAL BURDEN OF POOR DIETARY CHOICES AND TRENDS IS CONSERVATIVELY ESTIMATED TO BE $71 BILLION PER YEAR IN THE U.S. ALONE, REPRESENTING MEDICAL COSTS, PREMATURE DEATHS AND LOST PRODUCTIVITY.

USDA ECONOMIC RESEARCH SERVICE, 1999

CALORIE RESTRICTION (CR) IS A LIFELONG DIETARY STRATEGY AIMED AT INCREASING LIFE SPAN UP TO 65% BY LIMITING CALORIC INTAKE BY 25-60%.

JOURNAL OF NUTRITION, 1986

AN E.U. COW IS SUBSIDISED ABOUT $2.50 PER DAY, A JAPANESE COW IS SUBSIDISED ABOUT $7 PER DAY, AND YET 75% OF SUB-SAHARAN AFRICANS LIVE ON LESS THAN $2 PER DAY.

THE INTERNATIONAL DEVELOPMENT RESEARCH CENTRE,
GOVERNMENT OF CANADA, 2003

IN THE U.K. 1/3 OF FOOD BOUGHT IS THROWN OUT AS WASTE, A VALUE OF £10.2 BILLION PER YEAR.

WRAP (WASTE & RESOURCES ACTION PROGRAMME), 2008

THE TRANSPORTATION OF U.K. FOOD ACCOUNTED FOR AN ESTIMATED 30 BILLION VEHICLE KILO- METRES (19 BILLION MILES) IN 2002.

DEFRA (DEPARTMENT FOR ENVIRONMENT, FOOD AND RURAL AFFAIRS), 2005

A SURVEY SHOWED 50% OF U.K. RETAIL CHICKEN IS CONTAMINATED WITH CAMPYLOBACTER.

FOOD STANDARDS AGENCY, 2003

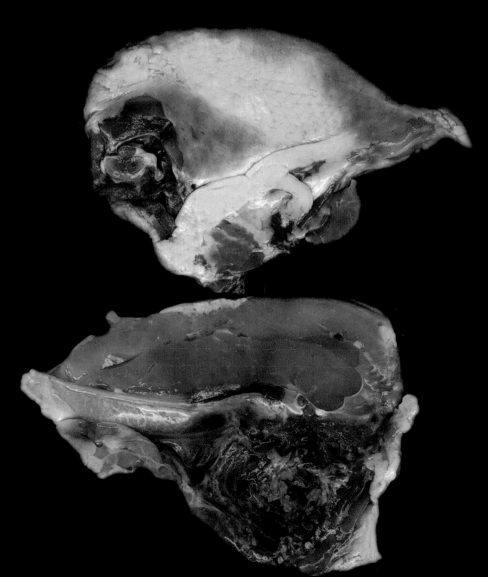

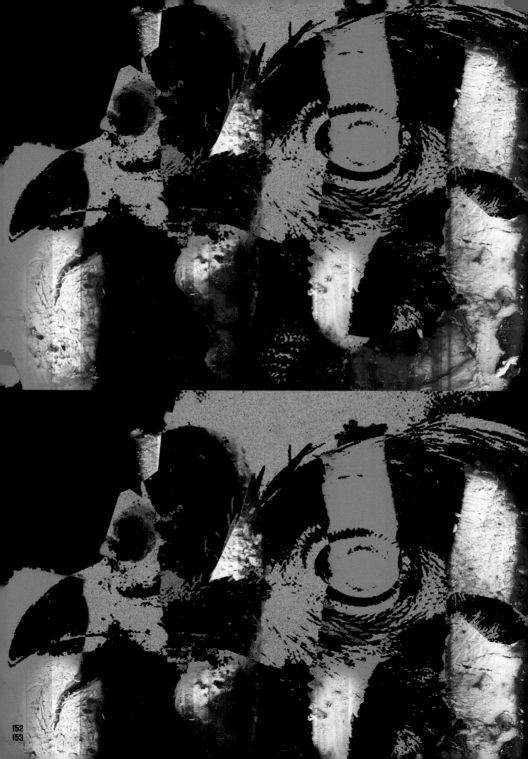

THE INTENSIVE RAISING OF CHICKENS IS ASSOCIATED WITH MANY SERIOUS WELFARE CONCERNS SUCH AS EXTREMELY HIGH STOCKING DENSITIES, FEED RESTRICTION, BEAK TRIMMING AND FORCED MOULTING.

ANIMAL SCIENCE DEPARTMENT, ULUDAĞ UNIVERSITY, TURKEY, 2006

AMERICAN FARMERS' SHARE OF THE AVERAGE FOOD DOLLAR HAS DROPPED BY 44% SINCE 1982.

USDA ECONOMIC RESEARCH SERVICE, 2006

MORE THAN 335 MILLION TONS OF MANURE ARE PRODUCED EACH YEAR AT ANIMAL FEEDING OPERATIONS IN THE U.S.

UNITED STATES DEPARTMENT OF AGRICULTURE, 2006

BIOSOLIDS REFER TO SEWAGE SLUDGE THAT HAS BEEN TREATED AND THEN SOLD AS FERTILISER, OFTEN STILL CONTAINING PATHOGENS AND CONTAMINANTS.

NATIONAL RESEARCH COUNCIL, 2002

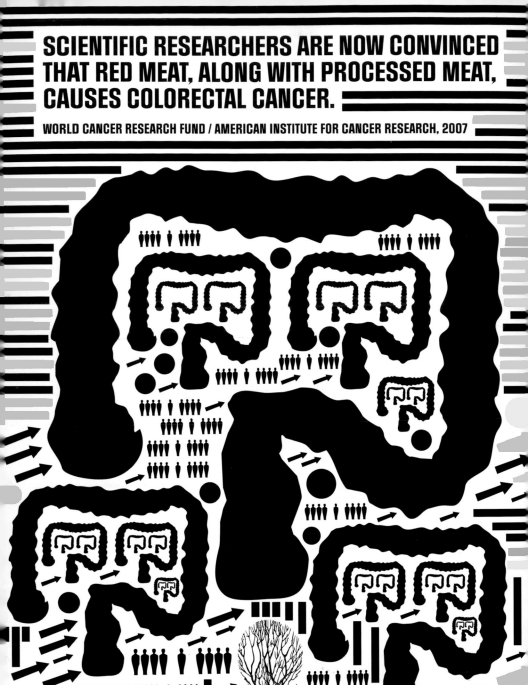

SCIENTIFIC RESEARCHERS ARE NOW CONVINCED THAT RED MEAT, ALONG WITH PROCESSED MEAT, CAUSES COLORECTAL CANCER.

WORLD CANCER RESEARCH FUND / AMERICAN INSTITUTE FOR CANCER RESEARCH, 2007

VITAMIN D IS NOW BEING THOUGHT OF AS AN EFFECTIVE MEANS OF PROTECTION AGAINST MULTIPLE SCLEROSIS.

CURRENT MEDICINAL CHEMISTRY, 2008

STROKE DAMAGE TO THE BRAIN CAN BE REDUCED BY A DIET HIGH IN SPINACH, BLUEBERRIES AND SPIRULINA.

EXPERIMENTAL NEUROLOGY, 2005

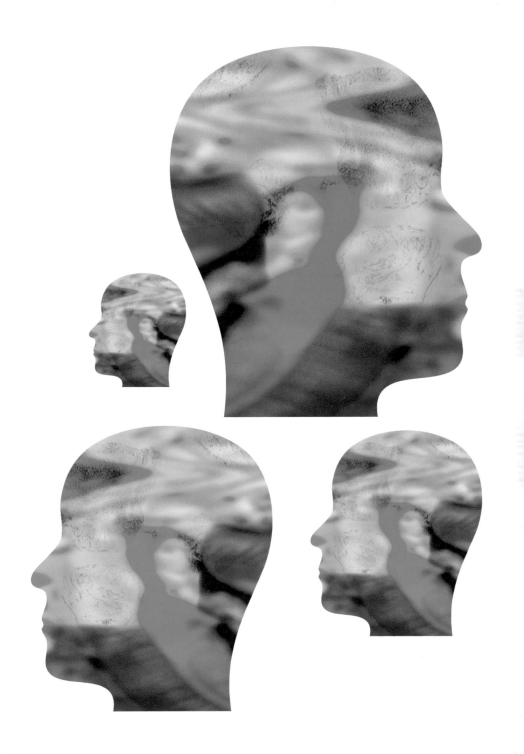

COCONUT OIL HAS BEEN MUCH SLANDERED, YET COMMUNITIES WHICH DERIVE MOST OF THEIR FAT CALORIES FROM COCONUT OIL ARE UNFAMILIAR WITH HEART DISEASE.

THE AMERICAN JOURNAL OF CLINICAL NUTRITION, 1981

DARK CHOCOLATE IS NOT ONLY VERY
HIGH IN ANTIOXIDANTS, BUT IT CAN ALSO
LOWER BLOOD PRESSURE AND HELP
WITH INSULIN SENSITIVITY.

THE AMERICAN JOURNAL OF CLINICAL NUTRITION, 2005

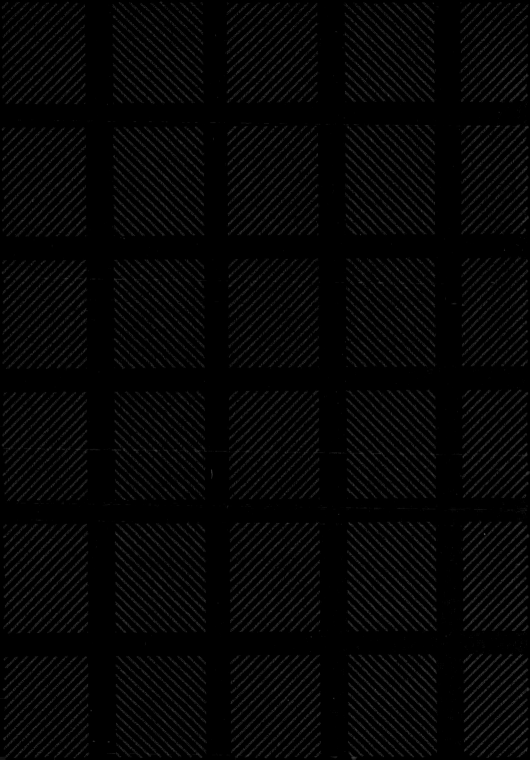

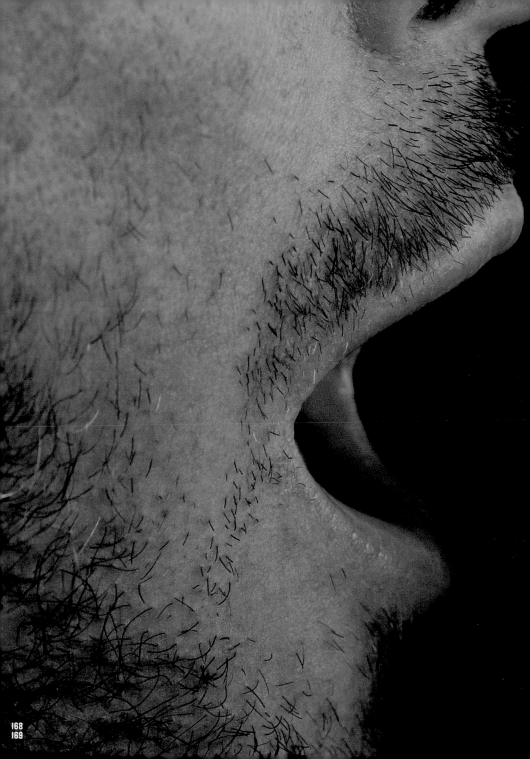

IN LONDON ALONE 6.9 MILLION TONS OF FOOD IS CONSUMED IN A GIVEN YEAR, AND 81% OF IT IS IMPORTED FROM OUTSIDE THE U.K.

CHARTERED INSTITUTION OF WASTES MANAGEMENT, 2002

A U.S. STUDY SHOWED CARROTS CAN TRAVEL 1,838 MILES (2,958 KM) TO REACH THE PLATE, HOWEVER IF THEY'RE SOURCED LOCALLY THEY ONLY TRAVEL 27 MILES (43 KM), ALMOST 70 TIMES LESS.

LEOPOLD CENTER FOR SUSTAINABLE AGRICULTURE, 2003

HIGH BLOOD PRESSURE, OR HYPERTENSION, CAN BE REDUCED BY EATING CELERY.

SCIENCE NEWS, 1992

CRANBERRY JUICE IS EFFECTIVE IN REDUCING OR ELIMINATING THE INCIDENCE OF URINARY TRACT INFECTIONS.

THE CANADIAN JOURNAL OF UROLOGY, 2002

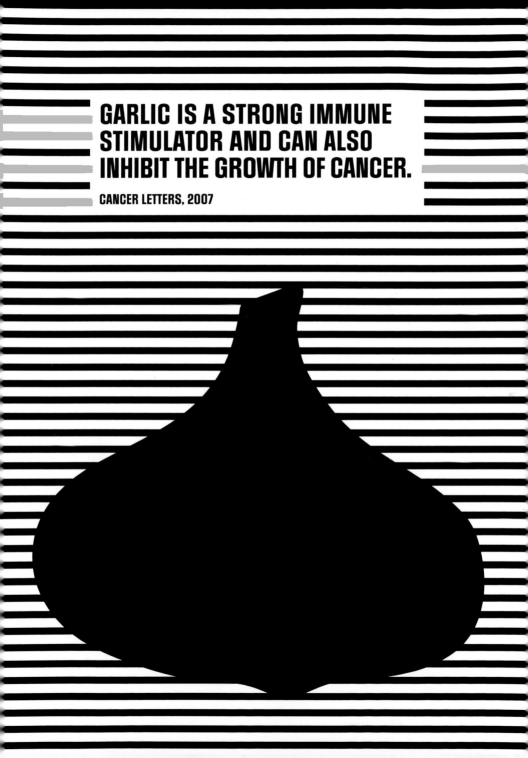

GARLIC IS A STRONG IMMUNE STIMULATOR AND CAN ALSO INHIBIT THE GROWTH OF CANCER.

CANCER LETTERS, 2007

ONE OUT OF EVERY FOUR CHILDREN UNDER FIVE—OR 146 MILLION CHILDREN—IN THE DEVELOPING WORLD IS UNDERWEIGHT FOR HIS OR HER AGE.

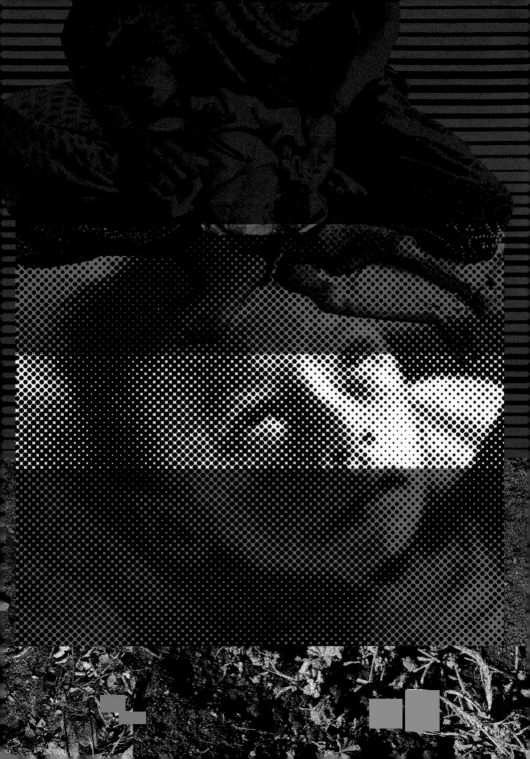

CITATIONS/FOOTNOTES

P. 08-09 There are currently 923 million starving people in the world.

Briefing Paper: "Hunger on the Rise." Food and Agriculture Organization of the United Nations. (Geneva: FAO, September 2008). Online: **www.fao.org/newsroom/common/ecg/1000923/en/hungerfigs.pdf**

In the last couple of decades progress had been made in reducing the proportion of starving people in the developing world from 20% down to just above 16% of the population. Sadly, that downward trend has now been reversed and this is primarily due to the recent dramatic rise in food prices. In the last two years the number of starving people has increased by 75 million.

P. 10-11 Chinese meat consumption per person has more than doubled since 1995, from 25 kg (55 lb) per person to 53 kg (117 lb).

Lane, J. "Meat vs. Fuel: Grain use in the U.S. and China, 1995–2008." *Biofuels Digest.* (April 2008). Online: **http://www.biofuelsdigest.com/MeatvsFuel.pdf**

Behind this increase are a couple of trends. Firstly, as in many other parts of the world, the Chinese are moving from the country into the cities. In turn, urbanized living has led to better job opportunities and increased affluence, while higher incomes and convenient shopping opportunities have translated into increased meat consumption. In the next few years, China will no longer be able to self-sufficiently produce the grain needed to feed its livestock. Once this happens there will be a dramatic hike in worldwide demand for grains, and a resulting significant price increase as well

P. 12-13 Global food prices have risen by 130% since 2002, and biofuel production is responsible for 75% of that increase.

Mitchell, D. "A Note on Rising Food Prices." The World Bank, Development Prospects Group: Policy Research Working Paper. 4682 (July 2008). Online: **http://econ. worldbank.org/external/default/main?pagePK=6416 5259&theSitePK=469372&piPK=64165421&menuPK =64166093&entityID=000020439_20080728103002**

Rising food prices aren't as serious an issue for developed countries where the income percentage spent on food is relatively low. However, in developing countries half of a family's income is on average spent on feeding itself. To make matters worse, the grains that typically sustain developing nations have recently doubled in price. This has become a difficult burden to bear, leading to riots and unrest as the number of starving people increases, and biofuel can largely be blamed for diverting the production of staple foods to ethanol and biodiesel production. There are also other contributing factors such as rising energy prices translating into higher transportation costs. This serious situation has led some to question government policies that actually provide incentives for producing

biofuels at the expense of the starving peoples of the world.

P. 14-15 Two-thirds of Americans are overweight or obese.

"Prevalence of Overweight and Obesity Among Adults: United States, 2003–2004." National Health and Nutrition Examination Survey (NHANES): Centers for Disease Control and Prevention. (Hyattsville, MD: National Center for Health Statistics, 2006). Online: **http://www.cdc.gov/nchs/fastats/overwt.htm**

This statistic has been increasing steadily since the early 1960s. Back then only 45% of the population was overweight or obese. This represents an increase of 47% since then. Even more shocking is the fact that this group of people is also becoming synonymous with low-income status. In the beginning of this time period less than 50% of this group was below the poverty level, and now 64% of this overweight population is below the poverty level.

P. 16-17 More than half of supermarket multi-buy promotions are for high-fat or high-sugar foods, despite the fact that health advice dictates these should not make up more than 7% of our diet.

Yates, L. "Cut-price, what cost? How supermarkets can affect your chances of a healthy diet." (London: National Consumer Council, 2008). Online: **http://www. sustainweb.org/pdf/NC217rr_cutprice_what_cost.pdf**

Up to 63% of supermarket promotions have been based on fatty or sugary foods. This is a stark contrast to the campaigns featuring fruits and vegetables, which seem to range only between 8% and 16% of a given store's promotions. Finally, it's worth considering that multi-buy promotions may be contributing significantly to the obscene amount of food waste generated annually.

P. 18-19 More than 10 million children die every year and the underlying cause for most of these deaths is starvation.

Black, R.E., Morris, S.S., and Bryce, J.B. "Where and why are 10 million children dying every year?" *The Lancet.* 361.9376 (2003): 2226–34. Online: **http://www.thelancet.com/journals/lancet/article/ PIIS0140-6736(03)13779-8/fulltext#article_upsell**

This disturbing number still only represents children under the age of five years old. Of these 10 million deaths it has been estimated that more than half (53%) are attributable to starvation, leading to underweight status and malnutrition. As a result of their nutritional deficiencies these children don't have capable immune systems to ward off disease and regain health. Almost 4 million of these deaths occur in the first month of life. The leading causes of death for all of these children are diarrhoea, malaria, pneumonia, AIDS, and neonatal causes. Since more than half are related to undernutrition, it would suggest we are witnessing over 5 million preventable deaths of children under five years of age per annum.

P. 20-21 Lettuce has been known to receive 4 spray rounds of insecticides, 2 spray rounds of fungicides, and 2 spray rounds of herbicides during its growth cycle.

Garthwaite, D.G., Thomas, M.R., and Dean, S. "Pesticide Usage Survey Report 163: Outdoor Vegetable Crops in Great Britain 1999." Department for Environment, Food and Rural Affairs (DEFRA) & Scottish Executive Environment and Rural Affairs Department. (2001). Online: **http://www.fera.defra.gov.uk/plants/pesticideUsage/outdoorveg1999.pdf**

The insecticides are used to control aphids and caterpillars. Fungicides are intended against botrytis, and herbicides against broad-leaved weeds. Exposure to such pesticides is known to have a direct impact on human health depending on which chemical family is used.

P. 22-23 In the United States more than 3,000 people die each year as a result of choking, mainly on food.

Online: **http://www2.redcross.org/services/hss/tips/choking.html**

Generally speaking, foods that are round, firm, hard to chew, or sticky are the most likely causes of a choking incident. The most risky foods in particular are hot dogs, hard candy, grapes, chewing gum, nuts, peanut butter, popcorn, and raw vegetables.

P. 24-25 Vitamin A deficiency will cause up to 500,000 children to go blind every year; half of them will die within a year of losing their sight.

Micronutrient deficiencies, WHO: **http://www.who.int/nutrition/topics/vad/en/**

Vitamin A deficiency is the leading cause of preventable blindness in children. A lack of this nutrient also increases the risk of disease and infection, since it plays a large role in regulating the immune system. All told, this deficiency is a problem in more than half of all countries, but especially in Africa and S.E. Asia. The tragic legacy is blindness, disease, and premature death, all of it needless. In order to help combat this alarming situation the World Health Organization (WHO) and its partners have conducted a vitamin A supplementation initiative, which has so far saved more than a million lives.

P. 26-27 Most people drink about 2 litres of water a day, but consume 3,000 litres a day if the water that goes into producing their food is taken into account.

"Running dry – Water for farming." *The Economist*. (September 18, 2008).

Farmers require a great deal of water to produce our food. Unfortunately, many of the world's farmers live in areas where water is considered scarce, such as northern China, southern Spain, and even the western U.S. Growing world populations will make this situation dramatically worse in the coming years. Exacerbating the problem even further are the recent patterns of global warming, which are creating permanent droughts in some parts of the world. Put together, this may lead us to believe that our current food crisis is more likely a water crisis.

P. 28-29 In the United States livestock consumes more than 7 times as much grain as is consumed directly by the country's entire human population.

Pimentel, D., and Pimentel, M. "Sustainability of meat-based and plant-based diets and the environment." *American Journal of Clinical Nutrition*. 78.3. (2003): 660S–663S. Online: **http://www.ajcn.org/cgi/content/full/78/3/660S#FN2**

With the global population already at unsustainable levels and forecast to grow even further, this survey assessed the different production energy requirements of meat-based diets versus plant-based diets. It concluded the production of meat requires far more energy, land and water than the growing of crops, and therefore for future sustainability a lactovegetarian diet was the best option. In fact, according to the U.S. Department of Agriculture's *Agricultural Statistics* published in 2001, the amount of grains fed annually to livestock in the United States would adequately feed 840 million people.

P. 30-31 One in three Africans are malnourished and about half of the continent's nearly 700 million people live on less than $1 a day.

Karanja, D.D., and McNeil, M.R. "African Agriculture – A Crucial Lifeline. Agriculture in the Global Economy – Hunger 2003." 13th Annual Report on the State of World Hunger. (Washington, DC: Bread for the World Institute, 2003). Online: **http://www.bread.org/learn/hunger-reports/hunger-report-pdfs/hunger-report-2003/chapter-4.pdf**

Although Africa's history of malnutrition and starvation has been a consistent one, the past thirty years have seen it worsen. Some would lay a portion of the blame on the doorstep of the richer nations which impose trade penalties against African goods and produce coming into their countries. Rather than supporting an already-disadvantaged trading partner, the wealthier nations are choosing to protect their own industries. While this type of trade policy is not the only contributing factor to the continent's woes, a fair and equitable international playing field would go a long way toward helping Africa help itself.

P. 32-33 Conditions like depression and bipolar disorder can be relieved by consuming Omega-3 fatty acids, found in oily fish like salmon.

Freeman, M.P., et al. "Omega-3 Fatty Acids: Evidence Basis for Treatment and Future Research in Psychiatry." *Journal of Clinical Psychiatry*. 67.12 (2006): 1954–67.

Omega-3 supplementation represents a valuable intervention in cases of mood disorders, but that isn't the only health benefit it can provide.

Specifically, it can help reduce cardiovascular risk in the areas of triglycerides and plaque growth. There's also a suggestion that it can help with gastrointestinal illnesses, risk of cancer, and brain health. Finally, it's also been shown that children with ADHD may benefit both behaviourally and thereby academically from omega-3 fatty acid supplementation.

P. 34-35 Based on current trends, the global fishing industry will be in a state of complete collapse by 2048.

Worm, B., et al. "Impacts of Biodiversity Loss on Ocean Ecosystem Services." *Science*. 314.5800 (2006): 787–90.

Currently 29% of the world's fish species are already considered to be in a state of collapse. This means that the catch is less than 10% of the recorded maximum. Despite this dire state of affairs, it has been suggested that immediate and drastic action could reverse this trend.

P. 36-37 The antioxidants that are abundant in fruits, vegetables and tea are valuable to us because they provide a longer life, reduced cancer risk, and lower the incidence of cardiovascular disease.

Rice-Evans, C., and Miller, N.J. "Antioxidants – the case for fruit and vegetables in the diet." *British Food Journal*. 97.9 (1995): 35–40

One of the theories about aging holds that we decline over time due to an accumulation of oxidative stress. Sources of oxidative stress include the byproducts of our bodies' metabolism along with free radicals that we ingest, through for example hydrogenated oils. How well our bodies deal with oxidative stress is directly connected to our antioxidant levels. Antioxidant nutrients are vitamin C, vitamin E, and beta-carotene, all of which are abundant in fruits and vegetables. There are also high levels of antioxidants in tea and red wine. It should come as no surprise, then, that vitamin E supplementation (for at least 2 years) reduces coronary heart disease risk by 40%. Further, the quarter of the population that eats the least fruits and vegetables has twice the risk of cancer. Antioxidants are not only helpful against cancer and cardiovascular disease, but also against cataracts and brain degeneration.

P. 38-39 You can protect against age-related macular degeneration by eating foods high in lutein and zeaxanthin such as corn, peppers, eggs, kiwi fruit, grapes, and zucchini (courgette).

Sommerburg, O., et al. "Fruits and vegetables that are sources for lutein and zeaxanthin: the macular pigment in human eyes." *British Journal of Ophthalmology*. 82 (1998): 907–10. Online: **http://www.pubmedcentral.nih.gov/articlerender.fcgi?artid=1722697**

Age-related macular degeneration (AMD) is the leading cause of blindness for those over 65 in the western hemisphere. Maintaining macular pigment is the only known protection against AMD. It is best augmented through diet, specifically by the consumption of fruits and vegetables. The increasing longevity of the aging population will heighten the importance of combating AMD in the coming years.

P. 40-41 Tomatoes, especially cooked tomatoes, can protect against prostate cancer.

Gann, P.H., et al. "Lower Prostate Cancer Risk in Men with Elevated Plasma Lycopene Levels: Results of a Prospective Analysis." *Cancer Research*. 59.6 (1999): 1225–30. Online: **http://cancerres.aacrjournals.org/cgi/reprint/59/6/1225**

Lycopene is the ingredient in tomatoes that provides this health benefit. The relationship is a strong and clear one, which shows a reduction in the risk of prostate cancer of up to 30%. It also seems capable of slowing the progression of the cancer. Lycopene is beneficial for other cancers as well, in particular stomach, colon, and possibly pancreatic tumours.

P. 42-43 Food colourings and additives increase hyperactivity in children.

McCann, D., et al. "Food additives and hyperactive behaviour in 3-year-old and 8/9-year-old children in the community: a randomized, double-blinded, placebo-controlled trial." *The Lancet*. 370.9598 (2007): 1560–67.

These conclusions are the result of a study that included both preschool and middle-school children. The children's diets eliminated colourings and additives for some time before the study began. For a number of succeeding weeks they were then given drinks containing various amounts of food colouring, including drinks containing none. All of the participants were "blind" as to which drinks contained colouring and additives and which didn't. Parents and teachers were then questioned about their observations regarding the hyperactivity of the children. The conclusion of the study determined that food colouring and additives increases hyperactivity in both preschool and middle-school aged children.

P. 44-45 Every year in the United States, up to 25 million pounds (11.3 million kg) of antimicrobial drugs (antibiotics, antivirals, antifungals and antiparasitics) are fed to livestock for nontherapeutic purposes.

Mellon, M., Benbrook, C., and Benbrook, K.L. "Hogging It: Estimates of Antimicrobial Abuse in Livestock." Union of Concerned Scientists. (January 2001). Online: **http://www.ucsusa.org/assets/documents/food_and_agriculture/hog_chaps.pdf**

The spectre of creating antibiotic-resistant microbes is virtually unavoidable when animals and humans are given the same antimicrobials, particularly the ones that are of most importance in human medicine.

This risk is magnified enormously when you consider the sheer volume of the pharmaceuticals being used. Reliable data is sketchy, despite the fact that these statistics are of exceptional importance. The best, most recent data calculated by the Union of Concerned Scientists indicates that 25 million pounds (11.3 million kg) of antimicrobials – up to 70% of the total produced annually in the U.S. – are fed to livestock each year for non-therapeutic purposes. This dwarfs the 3 million pounds (1.4 million kg) that are estimated to be used annually in human medicine.

P. 46-47 Eating at fast-food restaurants two or more times a week is strongly associated with weight gain and insulin resistance, leading to an increased risk of obesity and type 2 diabetes.

Pereira, M.A., et al. "Fast-food Habits, Weight Gain, and Insulin Resistance (The CARDIA Study): 15-Year Prospective Analysis". *The Lancet.* 365.9453 (2005): 36–42.

The consumption of fast-food has dramatically increased over the last three decades and The Coronary Artery Risk Development in Young Adults (CARDIA) study was one of the first scientific long-term studies to prove a direct correlation between the intake of fast-food with weight-gain and type 2 diabetes. It found that over a 15 year period, those who ate fast-food two or more times a week compared to once a week had gained an extra ten pounds and had a two-fold greater increase in insulin resistance. It also found that fast-food frequency was lowest for white women (about 1.3 times per week), while for men and other ethnic groups the average was around twice a week.

P. 48-49 Americans spend 49% of their food dollars away from home.

Food, CPI, Prices, and Expenditures Briefing Report. Economic Research Service, U.S. Department of Agriculture. (2008). Online: **http://www.ers.usda. gov/Briefing/CPIFoodAndExpenditures/**

On a typical day in 2008, the U.S. restaurant industry generated $1.5 billion in sales according to the National Restaurant Association. This astonishing revenue is not a coincidence, as the majority of the adult population acknowledges that dining in restaurants forms an important part of their lifestyle.

P. 50-5I Americans spend $55 billion per year on weight loss products and services.

U.S. Weight Loss & Diet Control Market (9th Edition). Report number FS22. Marketdata Enterprises, Inc. (April 2007).

This burgeoning market includes food items such as diet drinks, artificial sweeteners, meal replacements, diet pills, low-calorie dinner entrées and low-carb foods. It also includes diet books, exercise videos, commercial diet center chains, weight-loss camps for children, prescription drugs, bariatricians (doctors specializing in obesity), and weight-loss surgery.

P. 52-53 In the developed world, people consume about 4.5 kg (10 LB) of food additives per year, jumping to 11.5 kg (25 LB) if you include their salt intake.

Ensminger, A.H., Ensminger, M.E., Konlande, J.E., and Robson, J.R.K. *The Concise Encyclopedia of Foods & Nutrition* (Boca Raton, Florida: CRC Press, 1994).

Chemical additives are added to food for a number of reasons. They are used to add or change the colour of a product. They can extend shelf life with the use of preservatives and antioxidants. Some chemicals are meant to change product texture by emulsifying, stabilising or thickening. One of the largest categories is that of flavourings, with 4,500 possible compounds in use. Flavour enhancers act by making you think that the food you're eating is tastier than it really is. Monosodium glutamate (MSG) is the most well known of these, with more than 500,000,000 kg (551,000 U.S. tons) of MSG added to our food each year. The amount of additives jumps dramatically again when the category of sweeteners is also taken into consideration. The 52 kg (115 pounds) of added sugar consumed by the average person per annum dwarfs the total of all the other additives combined.

P. 54-55 27% or 96 billion pounds (43 billion kg) of available food is wasted in the U.S. each year.

Kantor, L.S., et al. "Estimating and Addressing America's Food Losses." *Food Review.* Economic Research Service, U.S. Department of Agriculture. (1997).Online: **http://www.ers.usda.gov/Publications/FoodReview/ Jan1997/Jan97a.pdf**

Not all of this waste is recoverable. For example, diseased livestock have to be condemned at the slaughterhouse, and mouldy produce cannot be consumed. Nevertheless, there is certainly a squandering of valuable nourishment that takes place when we discard fruit and vegetables simply because they are blemished and considered unsaleable. If we could reduce this waste by even 5%, that would provide a day's food to 4 million people.

P. 56 Each year in the U.S. foodborne diseases result in 76 million illnesses, 325,000 hospitalisations and 5,000 deaths.

Mead, Paul S., et al. "Food-Related Illness and Death in the United States." Centers for Disease Control and Prevention. *Emerging Infectious Diseases.* 5.5 (1999): 607–625. Online: **http://www.cdc.gov/ncidod/eid/ Vol5no5/mead.htm**

Within the category of deaths due to foodborne disease, three pathogens figure prominently: Salmonella, Listeria, and Toxoplasma. The largest overall number of fatalities belongs to the 23 million illnesses blamed on Norwalk-like viruses. Following on from these three culprits are a further 2.5 million illnesses believed to be caused by Campylobacter.

P. 57 Drought currently ranks as the single most common cause of food shortages.

"The State of Food Insecurity in the World 2003." Food and Agriculture Organization of the United Nations (Rome: FAO, 2003). Online: **ftp://ftp.fao.org/docrep/fao/006/j0083e/j0083e00.pdf**

Water and food are inextricably linked. It's virtually impossible to grow food of any kind without water. So it's no surprise that Africa is not only the driest continent, but also has the highest degree of hunger. Irrigation of cropland can certainly help with this situation. In fact the 17% of global cropland that is irrigated produces 40% of the world's food. These successful crops can, in turn, provide income as well as sustenance. Irrigation, then, has the potential to dramatically alleviate both hunger and poverty.

P. 58-59 Natural disasters, such as floods and cyclones, are now happening at a rate of 400-500 per year, an increase from 125 in the early 1980s, causing untold devastation as they wipe out crops and add to the severe global hunger situation.

"Disaster Risk Reduction: 2007 Global Review." United Nations International Strategy for Disaster Reduction Secretariat (Geneva: UNISDR, 2007). Online: **www.preventionweb.net/files/1130_GlobalReview2007.pdf**

On average, these disasters used to affect 174 million people annually, however that number has now risen to around 254 million. Floods alone have multiplied by a factor of six since 1980. Each mini-calamity, though seemingly small, can eradicate food sources and contribute even further to the extreme poverty being felt in many of these geographical areas. For example, a slight increase in temperature can bring about a disastrous locust infestation, which can wipe out an entire crop. Climate change is resulting in extreme weather and unpredictable seasons. The potential impact is to massively increase global poverty as the poor of the world do not have the capacity to recover from these disasters very easily, if at all.

P. 60-61 In less than 20 years the proportion of food crises caused by humans has more than doubled, increasing from 15% to over 35%, with many of these emergencies triggered by conflict.

World Food Programme. "What Causes Hunger?" Online: **http://www.wfp.org/hunger**

Conflicts generate food crises in a few ways. Firstly, as has been experienced recently in Asia, Africa, and Latin America, fighting displaces people from their homes. These homes have either been destroyed or are no longer safe havens. Secondly, in a state of conflict food supplies can become a strategic weapon. Water wells and crop fields may be either mined or contaminated. Starvation is also used as a weapon by withholding food supplies and livestock until submission is achieved.

P. 62-63 The agribusiness sector spent in excess of $139 million lobbying the U.S. government in 2008.

The Center for Responsive Politics. Washington, DC. (2009). Online: **http://www.opensecrets.org/lobby/alphalist_indus.php**

This is the amount spent by companies in the hope that their favoured political party will enact legislation that best suits their best interests, which needless to say is not necessarily the same as the consumer's.

P. 64-65 The agriculture industry uses 1,200 million lb (545 million kg) of pesticides over the course of a year in the U.S. alone.

Kiely, T., etal. "Pesticides Industry Sales and Usage: 2000 and 2001 Market Estimates." Office of Prevention, Pesticides, and Toxic Substances, U.S. Environmental Protection Agency. EPA-733-R-04-001 (2004). Online: **http://www.epa.gov/oppbead1/pestsales/01pestsales/market_estimates2001.pdf**

Pesticide use has tripled in the previous 30 years, from a level of 400 million pounds (181 million kg) in the mid-1960s. The U.S. accounts for almost one third of world sales, or $11 billion. Although the agriculture industry is by far the largest group of pesticide users, 30% of the total is also sold to other commercial industries and into the home and garden market.

P. 66-67 A reduction in the mineral content of fruits and vegetables has been seen over time in the U.K., with declines of up to 80%.

Mayer, A-M. "Historical changes in the mineral content of fruits and vegetables." *British Food Journal.* 99.6 (1997): 207–11.

Possible reasons for this reduction could be due to inconsistencies in the measurement or sampling. It could also be the result of eating ever-increasing amounts of imported fruits and vegetables, whose growth history we know nothing about. It may also have something to do with the plant varieties that are currently being cultivated. The plant qualities chosen for breeding may have nothing to do with nutrition and more to do with hardiness during transportation or resistance to blemishes. Finally, it may be related to current agricultural practices, which have a strong reliance on fertilisers and pesticides and a reduced emphasis on the use of organic matter to provide soil nutrients. Whatever the reasons, it's becoming increasingly hard to meet our daily nutritional requirement from the conventional fruits and vegetables available to us.

P. 68-69 Breast-fed infants have lower rates of hospital admissions, ear infections, diarrhoea, rashes, allergies, and other medical problems than bottle-fed babies.

Williams, R.D., and Stehlin, I. "Breast Milk or Formula: Making the Right Choice for Your Baby." U.S. Food and

Drug Administration. *FDA Consumer Magazine*. (October 1995 and June 1996). Online: **http://www.fda.gov/fdac/reprints/breastfed.html**

There are a couple of reasons for the health advantages experienced by breast-fed babies. Firstly, about 80% of the cells in breast milk are cells that kill bacteria, fungi, and viruses. This immunity benefit means that breast-fed babies are protected from a number of illnesses such as bronchitis, influenza, pneumonia, and staphylococcal infections. Bottle-fed babies are not protected in this same way. Secondly, breast-fed babies have a nutritional advantage since human milk is inherently perfect for babies, and contains over 100 ingredients not found in infant formula.

P. 70-71 Phthalates are chemicals, used in consumer products and food packaging, which find their way into foods such as infant formula and baby food and are known to disrupt reproductive development.

Parks, L.G., et al. "The Plasticizer Diethylhexyl Phthalate Induces Malformations by Decreasing Fetal Testosterone Synthesis during Sexual Differentiation in the Male Rat." *Toxicological Sciences*. 58 (2000): 339–49. Online: **http://toxsci.oxfordjournals.org/cgi/content/abstract/58/2/339?ck=nck**

Phthalates are industrial chemicals that are used to make plastic products more flexible, amongst other things. They are not immediately toxic, but they do have some very undesirable health effects when ingested. They are known to affect the endocrine (hormone) system and are disruptive to male reproductive development. Some studies implicate them as factors in decreasing male fertility and increased testicular cancer. Phthalates are also used in many consumer products from toys to kitchen flooring. They can also be used in food packaging. The reality is that phthalates have made their way into our environment and are now found in our drinking water as well as in infant formula and baby food. Phthalates are also fat-soluble and so are sometimes found in fat-containing foods such as milk, cream, butter and cheese.

P. 72-73 27 million tons of fish are discarded as waste every year.

Alverson, D.L., et al. "A global assessment of fisheries bycatch and discards." Food and Agriculture Organization of the United Nations. *FAO Fisheries Technical Paper* No. 339 (Rome: FAO, 1994). Online: **http://www.fao.org/docrep/003/T4890E/T4890E00.htm**

This incredible amount of waste is the result of using fishing methods that catch unintended fish species along with the target catch – a phenomenon known as bycatch. Shrimp trawl fisheries are at the top of the discard list, since they account for one-third of the global average of 27 million tons. Trawling uses large weighted nets that are dragged across the ocean floor to capture the catch along with many other species. These discarded fish represent up to one-third of the world's total catch.

P. 74-75 In tropical areas, the bycatch-to-shrimp ratio can be roughly 10:1.

"Good Stuff? – Shrimp. A Behind-the-Scenes Guide to the Things We Buy." Worldwatch Institute. (2004). Online: **http://www.worldwatch.org/system/files/GS0000.pdf**

Shrimp trawlers operate by dragging huge cone-shaped nets called trawls across the seabed. They pick up everything lying in their wake and throw away all but the shrimp. Not only does this unnecessarily kill all the sea life that is unfortunate enough to find its way into their nets, but it also decimates the seabed as the nets are dragged along the bottom.

P. 76-77 Excitotoxins cause the neurons in our brain to excite themselves to death. They are a group of chemicals and food additives such as aspartame and MSG, and are commonly found in our food and drinks.

Blaylock, R.L. *Excitotoxins: The Taste That Kills* (Santa Fe, NM: Health Press, 1996).

Not only do excitotoxins such as aspartame and monosodium glutamate (MSG) cause such harm to our brains, they are also strongly linked to some of the worst neurodegenerative diseases such as Parkinson's disease, Alzheimer's disease, ALS (Lou Gehrig's disease), and Huntington's disease.

P. 78-79 Eating apples and onions can improve the inflammation associated with conditions like rheumatoid arthritis.

Guardia, T., et al. "Anti-inflammatory properties of plant flavonoids. Effects of rutin, quercetin and hesperidin on adjuvant arthritis in rat." *Farmaco*. 56 (2001): 683–87.

The reason these two foods are so helpful is because they contain high levels of quercetin. Quercetin is a compound that can improve many conditions involving free radicals and oxidative stress, for example arthritis can be relieved, as can some allergies. Quercetin also seems to boost the immune system, especially when the body is exposed to viruses.

P. 80-81 Blueberries can protect your brain from the effects of aging.

Lau, F.C., Shukitt-Hale, B., and Joseph, J.A. "The beneficial effects of fruit polyphenols on brain aging." *Neurobiology of Aging*. 26S (2005): 128–32.

As a group, fruits and vegetables are well known to reduce the cumulative effects of aging, with blueberries standing out as one of the best performers. The degeneration of brain function is believed to be the result of accumulated damage over time. Blueberries, however, are packed with the blue anthocyanin pigment, which is a powerful antioxidant that appears to protect, and maybe even reverse, some of this age-related brain damage.

P. 82-83 The rate of obesity amongst men in England has increased by 75% since 1993.

"Statistics on Obesity, Physical Activity and Diet: England, 2006." The Information Centre, Lifestyle Statistics, National Health Service. (2006). Online: **http://www.ic.nhs.uk/webfiles/publications/opan06/OPAN%20bulletin%20finalv2.pdf**

In 1993 the proportion of English men classified as obese was 13% of the population. Just over a decade later, this ratio grew to 23%. As a comparison, there is a larger prevalence of obesity in the U.S. (32%), but the current rate of increase is much higher in England.

P. 84-85 About 280,000 Americans die every year as a direct result of being overweight.

Allison, D.B., et al. "Annual Deaths Attributable to Obesity in the United States." *Journal of the American Medical Association*. 282 (1999): 1530–38. Online: **http://jama.ama-assn.org/cgi/reprint/282/16/1530?maxtoshow=&HITS=10&hits=10&RESULTFORMAT=1&author1=Allison&andorexacttitle=and&andorexacttitleabs=and&andorexactfulltext=and&searchid=1&FIRSTINDEX=0&sortspec=relevance&resourcetype=HWCIT**

Obesity results in increased risk and incidence of a number of potentially deadly health diagnoses. The most common are hypertension (high blood pressure), type 2 diabetes, heart disease and stroke. Not quite as deadly are health threats relating to gall bladder disease, high blood cholesterol, insulin resistance and glucose intolerance.

P. 86-87 Globally, each year more than 56 billion animals are raised as livestock for slaughter.

Food and Agriculture Organization of the United Nations. FAOSTAT Statistical Database. (2008). Online: **http://faostat.fao.org/**

It is also forecast that by 2050 we will see this number double, since demand is increasing by 2%-4% each year. Most of these animals are raised on factory farms, where living conditions are appalling, if not inhumane.

P. 88-89 It takes 100,000 litres of water to produce 1 kilogram of beef.

Pimentel, D., and Pimentel, M. *Food, Energy and Society* (Niwot, CO: Colorado University Press, 1996).

Compared to the 3,500 litres required to produce 1 kilogram of chicken, raising beef cattle is a very expensive use of water resources. It becomes even more extravagant when compared to the 900 litres required for a kilogram of wheat. These numbers are not just the amount of water the animals drink, but also the amount required to grow the grain necessary to raise the livestock.

P. 90-91 18% of global greenhouse gas emissions are attributable to livestock production—more than the transportation sector.

Steinfeld, H., et al. "Livestock's Long Shadow." The Livestock, Environment and Development (LEAD) Initiative, Food and Agriculture Organization of the United Nations. (2006). Online: **http://www.fao.org/docrep/010/a0701e/a0701e00.htm**

This startling statistic is measured using a CO_2 equivalency scale and takes into account different activities, including the cutting down of forests to provide more pasture, the burning of fossil fuels to make fertilisers for feed production, and the release of methane gas from animal digestion. Livestock production takes up over 70% of all agricultural land, and 30% of the total land on the planet. The moral of this survey is that you can help the environment by simply eating less meat.

P. 92-93 Grass-fed, organically raised cows produce milk and beef that have significantly higher amounts of omega-3 fatty acids, vitamin E and other important nutrients.

Bergamo, P., et al. "Fat-soluble vitamin contents and fatty acid composition in organic and conventional Italian dairy products." *Food Chemistry*. 82.4 (2003): 625–31.

This comparison was made against conventional grain-fed beef. Typically, cows are fed cereals, corn and protein supplements. Grass-fed cows receive, however, their nutrient advantages from the forage-based diet that is more natural to them. This means they eat fresh or preserved grass and clover. Organic milk products and grass-fed beef are a good source of omega-3 fatty acids and antioxidants, and can therefore provide significant health benefits over the same conventional products. A matchbox-sized piece of organic cheese can provide up to 88% of the RDI for omega-3 fatty acids.

P. 94-95 Broccoli, and its family of cruciferous vegetables, contains sulforaphane, which has been proven to inhibit the growth of breast cancer.

Jackson, S.J.T., and Singletary, K.W. "Sulforaphane Inhibits Human MCF-7 Mammary Cancer Cell Mitotic Progression and Tubulin Polymerization." *Journal of Nutrition*. 134 (2004): 2229–36. Online: **http://jn.nutrition.org/cgi/reprint/134/9/2229?maxtoshow=&HITS=10&hits=10&RESULTFORMAT=&fulltext=sulforaphane&searchid=1&FIRSTINDEX=0&sortspec=relevance&resourcetype=HWCIT**

Broccoli and the other cruciferous vegetables are helpful against cancer in a number of ways. Firstly, they stimulate our bodies to produce enzymes, which can destroy carcinogens. Secondly, they help prevent normal healthy cells from becoming cancerous. Finally, they help slow tumor growth. These valuable health benefits are not only evident for breast cancer, but also for colon cancer. In fact, those eating a significant amount of broccoli regularly are thought to have a 50% less likely chance of developing colon cancer. Besides broccoli, the cruciferous family of vegetables also includes arugula, bok choy, brussels sprouts, cabbage, cauliflower, kale, radishes, rutabaga and turnips.

P. 96-97 Curcumin, a compound in turmeric and curry powder, stops the growth of certain cancer cells and protects the brain against Parkinson's disease.

Jiang, M-C., et al. "Curcumin induces apoptosis in immortalized NIH 3T3 and malignant cancer cell lines." *Nutrition and Cancer*. 26.1 (1996): 111–20.

Curcumin is found in the intensely yellow spice known as turmeric. Well known in Chinese as well as Ayurvedic medicine, it has historically been used as an antiseptic for cuts and bruises, an anti-inflammatory for conditions such as arthritis, and as a detoxifying agent to help purify the body. The scientific world is interested in curcumin because it is proving to be effective in keeping cancer at bay, as well as protecting the liver. Its anti-cancer properties seem to revolve around inhibiting either the size and/or number of tumours. The types of cancer where it is showing promise are skin, colon, kidney and liver cancer.

P. 98-99 Resveratrol, an ingredient in red grapes, red grape juice and red wine, has been shown to have significant beneficial effects on cholesterol levels.

Castilla, P., et al. "Concentrated red grape juice exerts antioxidant, hypolipidemic, and anti-inflammatory effects in both hemodialysis patients and healthy subjects." *American Journal of Clinical Nutrition*. 84 (2006): 252–62. Online: **http://www.ajcn.org/cgi/reprint/84/1/252**

Specifically, resveratrol has been shown to reduce levels of LDL (the "bad" cholesterol), increase levels of HDL (the "good" cholesterol), and decrease the inflammation that is usually associated with cardiovascular disease. Resveratrol is also seemingly capable of inhibiting certain cancers, in particular skin and prostate cancer. As if that wasn't beneficial enough, resveratrol has also been shown to protect against obesity-linked health risks and appears to exhibit neuroprotective effects.

P. 100-101 Bottled water has been found to be no different than tap water, containing the same contaminants but at 1,900 times the price.

Naidenko, O., et al. "Bottled Water Quality Investigation: 10 Major Brands, 38 Pollutants." Environmental Working Group. (October 2008). Online: **http://www.ewg.org/reports/bottledwater**

In these independent tests a total of 38 contaminants were found, with an average of 8 contaminants per brand. Some brands were chemically indistinguishable from tap water, and even bore the chemical residues

of water treatment facilities. Among the chemicals found were known carcinogens, heavy metals such as arsenic, and fertiliser residue. In fact, some of the samples analysed exceeded the legal limits for contaminants. Consumers are provided with tap water analysis results on an annual basis; the bottled water industry however, is not required to disclose the results of its testing.

P. 102-103 Agriculture accounts for more than 70% of the world's total water use.

"Coping with water scarcity: Challenge of the twenty-first century." UN-Water and the Food and Agriculture Organization of the United Nations. (22 March 2007). Online: **http://www.fao.org/nr/water/docs/escarcity.pdf**

Already an alarming statistic, it's made even more daunting in the face of increasing water-related challenges. These pressures can be attributed to an increasing population that is also becoming more urbanised. Urbanisation is usually accompanied by a shift in food consumption toward water-intensive food, such as meat. On the supply side, there are also concerns about climate change and its impact, along with water quality issues related to pollution.

P. 104-105 Agriculture is responsible for 70% of the water pollution in the United States.

Statement of Michael Cook, Director, Office of Wastewater Management, before the Subcommittee on Livestock, Dairy, and Poultry and the Subcommittee on Forestry, Resource Conservation and Research of the Committee on Agriculture, U.S. House of Representatives. (13 May 1998). Reducing Water Pollution from Animal Feeding Operations. Online: **http://www.epa.gov/ocirpage/hearings/testimony/105_1997_1998/051398.htm**

Fertiliser run-off from crop production is responsible for more than half the cases of polluted areas. This type of pollution disrupts the nutrient balance in the rivers and streams and as a result threatens their aquatic life. Manure from animal feeding operations is the next largest pollutant.

P. 106-107 Pregnant mothers who eat contaminated fish will increase the chance of having children with lower IQs along with memory and attention issues.

Jacobson, J.L., and Jacobson, S.W. "Intellectual Impairment in Children Exposed to Polychlorinated Biphenyls in Utero." *The New England Journal of Medicine*. 335 (1996): 783–89. Online: **http://content.nejm.org/cgi/contentabstract/335/11/783**

These cognitive deficits are related to the amount of fish consumed and the level of polychlorinated biphenyls (PCBs) contamination. The children who had the most exposure were three times as likely to have lower IQ scores, and were also twice as likely to be behind in reading comprehension. These impacts on intellectual functioning are thought to be long-term.

P. 108-109 The Gulf of Mexico contains an area of up to 20,000 km² (the size of New Jersey) referred to as a Dead Zone—so called because nothing can live there due to the oxygen-depletion caused by fertiliser run-off.

Rabalais, N.N., Turner, R.E., and Wiseman, Jr. W.J. "Hypoxia in the Gulf of Mexico." *Journal of Environmental Quality.* 30 (2001): 320–29. Online: **http://jeq. scijournals.org/cgi/reprint/30/2/320**

About 150 Dead Zones exist around the world. They are created when fertiliser run-off encourages an overabundance of algae to bloom. The algae life-cycle requires oxygen, and so it is depleted from the surrounding water. As a result of this any existing marine life is suffocated and the water cannot sustain any new life. The Dead Zone in the Gulf of Mexico is one of the largest and best known. It has been created by fertiliser run-off from the Mississippi River and has more than doubled in size since it was first measured in 1985. UNEP (U.N. Environment Programme) feels that reducing these nitrogen discharges, however, could restore the seas back to health. In fact, an example has already been set in Europe resulting in a 37% reduction of nitrates entering the North Sea.

P. 110-111 94% of survey respondents in the U.K. feel that all food containing genetically modified material should be labelled.

Poortinga, W., and Pidgeon, N.F. "Public Perceptions of Genetically Modified Food and Crops, and the GM Nation? Public Debate on the Commercialisation of Agricultural Biotechnology in the UK." Understanding Risk Working Paper 04-01. (Norwich: Centre for Environmental Risk, 2004). Online: **http://www.pgeconomics.co.uk/pdf/final_report_gm_survey_2003_04-02-06.pdf**

The purpose of this survey was to assess public attitudes toward genetically modified (GM) foods in the U.K. Strikingly, 79% of people felt that biotechnology companies should be made liable for any damage caused by GM products. Further, 84% of respondents believed that more information was needed before they would be able to form a clear opinion about GM foods.

P. 112-113 Mice fed genetically modified food experienced significantly reduced fertility.

Velimirov, A., Binter, C., and Zentek, J. "Biological effects of transgenic maize NK603xMON810 fed in long-term reproduction studies in mice." Austrian Agency for Health and Food Safety (AGES). (2008). Veterinärmedizinische Universität Wien (VUW). Online: **https://www.dafne.at/dafne_plus_homepage/download.php?t=ProjectReportAttachment&k=1292**

This study examined the cumulative, multi-generational effects of mice consuming GM feed, as compared to those eating unaltered food. After four generations the GM-fed group experienced reduced fertility and lower litter weights. These results are especially significant because GM crops are mostly fed to breeding livestock animals.

P. 114-115 Agricultural workers are twice as likely to die on the job as workers in other sectors.

"Agriculture mortality rates remain high." Press Release, International Labour Organization. (22 October 1997). Online: **http://www.ilo.org/global/About_the_ILO/Media_and_public_information/Press_releases/lang--en/WCMS_008027/index.htm**

Around the world, agricultural workers account for at least 170,000 of the total occupational deaths each year. This statistic represents half of all fatal accidents. These fatalities are primarily the result of incidents involving cutting tools and machinery, such as tractors and harvesters. Exposure to pesticides and other agrochemicals also contribute to the death toll. Workers in developing countries are particularly at risk since they may lack adequate education, training, health or safety systems. Unfortunately, these mortality rates remain high, despite decreases in fatal accidents in other dangerous occupations, such as mining and construction.

P. 116-117 Consumers worldwide spent £1.1 billion on Fairtrade-Certified Products in 2006, a 42% increase from the prevous year, which directly benefited over 7 million people in developing countries.

"7 Million Farming Families Worldwide Benefit as Global Fairtrade Sales Increase By 40% and UK Awareness Of The Fairtrade Mark Rises to 57%." Press Release, The Fairtrade Foundation. (10 August 2007). Online: **http://www.fairtrade.org.uk/press_office/press_releases_and_statements/archive_2007/aug_2007/global_fairtrade_sales_increase_by_40_benefiting_14_million_farmers_worldwide.aspx**

The millions that were helped by these Fairtrade sales were the farmers, workers and their families. The products they sold include cocoa, coffee, tea, bananas, and now cotton as well. Some large retailers are now embracing this trend by devoting complete product lines to Fairtrade-Certified commodities. The difference this has made to the lives of the producers and their families is not a small one. Not only are they receiving a fair price for their crops, but also one of the conditions of certification is a commitment to a long-term commercial relationship, which enables farmers to experience, often for the first time, financial stability for themselves and their families.

P. 118-119 Mushrooms, along with barley and oats, contain beta-glucans, which are able to stimulate the immune system to overcome bacterial, viral, fungal and parasitic infections.

Mantovani, M.S., et al. "Beta-Glucans in promoting health; Prevention against mutation and cancer." *Mutation Research.* 658.3 (2008): 154–61.

Beta-glucans are highly effective immune enhancers whose abilities to address some very serious conditions are impressive. They operate by stimulating the immune defences to identify and destroy foreign invaders. There is a range of cancerous conditions that are helped by beta-glucans such as prostate and kidney cancers. Progress is made against these diseases due to the destruction of tumour cells. Beyond these benefits, beta-glucans are also helpful with reducing post-operative infections, stubborn Methicillin-resistant Staphylococcus aureus (MRSA) infections, and respiratory infections. There have also been scientific studies that suggest beta-glucans may be helpful in combating antibiotic-resistant organisms and anthrax.

P. 120-121 Green tea is a very effective cancer inhibitor and preventer.

Ahmad, N., et al. "Green Tea Constituent Epigallo-catechin-3-Gallate and Induction of Apoptosis and Cell Cycle Arrest in Human Carcinoma Cells." *Journal of the National Cancer Institute*. 89.24 (1997): 1881–86. Online: **http://jnci.oxfordjournals.org/cgi/content/abstract/89/24/1881**

The polyphenol compounds in green tea are effective against cancer in that they stop cancer cells from growing and developing. Additionally, these compounds go one important step further by inducing cancer cells to undergo a programmed death sequence. This results in cancer cells killing themselves. While there are no certainties as to suggested amounts, 2–3 cups of green tea per day should contribute strongly toward these health benefits.

P. 122-123 Americans eat almost triple (167%) the amount recommended sugar, a source of 500 daily calories and 23% of the suggested caloric intake.

Kantor, L.S. "A Comparison of the U.S. Food Supply with the Food Guide Pyramid Recommendations." In: Frazão, E., ed. "America's Eating Habits: Changes and Consequences." USDA/ERS. AIB-750 (1999): 71–95. Online: **http://www.ers.usda.gov/Publications/AIB750/**

The suggested daily limit for sugar is the equivalent of 12 teaspoons. Americans, however, are consuming on average 32 teaspoons per day, almost triple the recommended total. This statistic is consistent with the sharp increase in the use of high-fructose corn syrup as a sweetener. In fact, HFCS now represents 40% of the sweeteners being consumed. One source of these sugar calories is soft drinks, which represents a conscious consumer choice. However, there is also an increasing incidence of these sweeteners ending up in processed foods that are not even meant to be sweet, such as crackers.

P. 124-125 Close to one quarter of the U.S. population suffers from a condition called metabolic syndrome, which results in an inability to process sugar.

Ford, E.S., Giles, W.H., and Dietz, W.H. "Prevalence of the Metabolic Syndrome Among U.S. Adults." *Journal of the American Medical Association*. 287.3 (2002): 356-59. Online: **http://jama.ama-assn.org/cgi/content/full/287/3/356**

The term "metabolic syndrome" describes a group of five symptoms that indicate higher risk for diabetes, heart disease, and strokes. It is also called Syndrome X, and Insulin Resistance Syndrome. This collection of measurements relates to blood sugar, cholesterol, blood pressure, waist circumference, and triglyceride levels. Since 90% of people diagnosed with type 2 diabetes are overweight, the importance of exercise and nutrition in preventing diabetes should not be underestimated. In the over-60 age group, the incidence of metabolic syndrome jumps to more than 40%.

P. 126-127 High-fructose corn syrup (HFCS), the sweetener used in most soft drinks and many processed foods, is metabolised directly into body fat.

Bray, G.A., Nielsen, S.J., and Popkin, B.M. "Consumption of high-fructose corn syrup in beverages may play a role in the epidemic of obesity." *American Journal of Clinical Nutrition*. 79 (2004): 537–43. Online: **http://www.ajcn.org/cgi/reprint/79/4/537.pdf**

HFCS is processed differently in the body than other types of sugar. Firstly, it is sent directly to the liver to be turned into fat, rather than being burned as energy. Secondly, it does not stimulate the release of insulin. Blood sugar levels aren't brought down properly, contributing to insulin resistance. Finally, HFCS does not stimulate the release of leptin, a hormone messenger meant to restrict food intake. This will encourage overeating. All three of these factors can be direct contributors to obesity. In fact, the increasing pattern of HFCS consumption mirrors the obesity rates in the U.S.

P. 128-129 Increased consumption of sugar-sweetened drinks increases the likelihood of weight gain and the risk of type 2 diabetes.

Schulze, M.B., et al. "Sugar-Sweetened Beverages, Weight Gain, and Incidence of Type 2 Diabetes in Young and Middle-Aged Women." *Journal of the American Medical Association*. 292.8 (2004): 927-934. Online: **http://jama.ama-assn.org/cgi/content/abstract/292/8/927?ijkey=c80b1d6cb73eb16204c054a5d99f7a83f0e21e64&keytype2=tf_ipsecsha**

Soft drinks have become the largest single food source of calories in the U.S. diet. Sweetened drinks also supply a great deal of rapidly absorbable sugars. These sweeteners put great demand on insulin production, a risk factor for type 2 diabetes. This sugar impact is very significant since most adolescents consume soft drinks on a daily basis. This pattern is likely to be a strong contributing factor to the 100% rise in child obesity between 1980 and 1994, not to mention the affiliated increased risk of acquiring type 2 diabetes.

P. 130-131 Globally, there are 3 million cases of acute pesticide poisonings each year, resulting in 220,000 deaths.

Jeyaratnam, J. "Acute Pesticide Problem: A Major Health Problem." *World Health Statistics Quarterly*. 43.3

(1990): 139–44. Online: **www.communityipm.org/ toxictrail/Documents/Jeryaratnam-WHO1990.pdf**

These findings may even be underreported by half, since they only include poisonings reported to hospitals. In other words, there may be the same number again of unreported, milder intoxications. Buried in these numbers are suicides and attempted suicides, a number thought to be as high as 73% in some countries such as Malaysia. Another survey based on self-reporting in Asia estimates that there could be as many as 25 million pesticide poisonings each year. Clearly, this is a problem that requires involvement at all levels, particularly government, agrochemical industries, international agencies, and victims.

P. 132-133 Carbonated caffeinated drinks leach calcium from bones thereby contributing significantly to osteoporosis.

Heaney, R.P., and Rafferty, K. "Carbonated beverages and urinary calcium excretion." *American Journal of Clinical Nutrition*. 74.3 (2001): 343–47. Online: **http:// www.ajcn.org/cgi/content/abstract/74/3/343**

For many years nutritionists have believed there is a link between the intake of carbonated drinks and the increased risk of bone fractures. Robert Heaney and Karen Rafferty's study undertaken at the Creighton University Osteoporosis Research Center in Omaha, however, showed that although the phosphoric acid in carbonated drinks had a negligible effect on calcium levels, when fizzy drinks were caffeinated (ie. colas) they caused excess calciurua (calcium loss). In 2006, the Framingham Osteoporosis Study also confirmed that colas are associated with low bone mineral density (BMD) in women.

P. 134-135 Organic crops contain higher levels of important nutrients than conventionally grown crops.

Worthington, V. "Nutritional Quality of Organic Versus Conventional Fruits, Vegetables, and Grains." *Journal of Alternative and Complementary Medicine*. 7.2 (2001): 161–73. Online: **http://www.ioia.net/ images/pdf/orgvalue.pdf**

There is an immediately obvious benefit to eating organic fruits and vegetables just by avoiding the ingestion of pesticides. An even more important advantage is the fact that organically grown crops are higher in vitamin C, iron, magnesium, and phosphorus. The quality of essential amino acids is also superior in organic fruits, vegetables, and grains. Finally, organic crops contain lower amounts of heavy metals. It is important to note that, with regard to vitamin C, five servings of organic vegetables meet the recommended daily intake, whereas conventionally grown vegetables in some cases may not.

P. 136-137 Benzene, a toxic and carcinogenic chemical, has been found in soft drinks and other beverages having been formed by a mixture of their ingredients.

"Data on Benzene in Soft Drinks and Other Beverages – Data through May 16, 2007." U.S. Food and Drug Administration. CFSAN/Office of Food Additive Safety. (July 2007). Online: **http://www.cfsan.fda. gov/~dms/benzdata.html**

Two ingredients in soft drinks are able to chemically combine, forming benzene. The additives are benzoate salts and ascorbic acid (vitamin C). Warmer temperatures and light are the conditions that bring on the transformation. Benzene is not intended for human consumption due to its cancer-causing properties and poisonous effects.

P. 138-139 Once ingested, the artificial sweetener aspartame converts into formaldehyde, a toxic and carcinogenic substance, which then accumulates in tissues such as the liver, kidneys and brain.

Trocho, C., et al. "Formaldehyde Derived from Dietary Apsartame Binds to Tissue Components In Vivo." *Life Sciences*. 63.5 (1998): 337–49. Online: **http://www. sweetpoison.com/pdf/Trochostudy.pdf**

Formaldehyde is the preservative used by funeral homes for embalming human remains. Not only is there a chemical transformation that helps to convert aspartame to toxic formaldehyde but this effect is cumulative. In other words, the body is not able to rid itself of the formaldehyde effectively and it's seemingly capable of binding to tissues and accumulating there. Aspartame is also being blamed for many other serious ailments, many of them neurological, such as seizures, brain tumours, dementia, migraines, brain lesions, MS-like symptoms, memory loss and confusion.

P. 140-141 In America, 63% of Saturday morning TV advertising, mostly aimed at children, is for food products. A third of these adverts are for high-sugar cereals, and the rest for food with overall poor nutritional value.

Gamble, M., and Cotugna, N. "A Quarter Century of TV Food Advertising Targeted at Children." *American Journal of Health Behavior*. 23.4 (1999): 261–67.

Advertised food products are generally high-fat and/ or low-fibre and are not usually representative of the nutrition guidelines. The resounding message being repeated to children is one of inappropriate food choices. Some kids are watching up to three hours of commercials in a week, a significant amount of persuasion. The after-school advertising time slot of 3–6pm shows a similar lack of support for actual dietary guidelines and an inaccurate message about proper dietary choices. Research shows that there has been no improvement over the last 25 years in the quality of food being marketed to children.

P. 142-143 The financial burden of poor dietary choices and trends is conservatively estimated to be $71 billion per year in the U.S. alone,

representing medical costs, premature deaths and lost productivity.

Frazão, E. "High Costs of Poor Eating Patterns In the United States." In: Frazão, E., ed. "America's Eating Habits: Changes and Consequences." USDA/ERS. AIB-750 (1999): 5–32. Online: **http://www.ers.usda. gov/Publications/AIB750/**

This calculation is based on the four chronic health conditions, which account for more than half of all the deaths in the U.S. They are coronary heart disease, cancer, stroke and diabetes, all of which are increasingly linked to dietary patterns. This study notes that just by convincing the population to make healthy food choices the annual economy could be improved by up to $71 billion. Although this bottom line is a dramatic number, it does not even attempt to factor in the inestimable grief and anguish that would be avoided by reducing chronic diseases and premature deaths.

P. 144-145 Calorie Restriction (CR) is a lifelong dietary strategy aimed at increasing life span up to 65% by limiting caloric intake by 25-60%.

Weindruch, R., et al. "The Retardation of Aging in Mice by Dietary Restriction: Longevity, Cancer, Immunity and Lifetime Energy Intake." *Journal of Nutrition.* 116.4 (1986): 641–54. Online: **http://jn.nutrition. org/cgi/reprint/116/4/641**

Calorie Restriction (CR) is meant to limit calorie intake but not nutrition. Not only does CR increase life span, but it also delays the onset of diseases such as kidney disease, diabetes, autoimmune diseases, and neurological dysfunctions. How calorie restriction helps to achieve this longevity is not well understood. One theory is that CR reduces the build-up of oxidative stress in the body. Since higher levels of oxidative stress are associated with symptoms of aging, this sounds plausible. Another train of thought relates to the fact that we often see toxins stored in fat cells. With CR, there is less body fat, so fewer storage compartments, less build-up of toxins, and a sustained higher level of long-term health. Finally, a simplified theory holds that our bodies are only designed to process a certain number of lifetime calories, and so if you eat less you can spread them out over a longer time frame.

P. 146-147 An E.U. cow is subsidised about $2.50 per day, a Japanese cow is subsidised about $7 per day, and yet 75% of sub-Saharan Africans live on less than $2 per day.

Medhora, R. "Viewpoint: tariffs and trade liberalisation in developing countries." (Quote attributed to Nicholas Stern, one-time World Bank Chief Economist.) The International Development Research Centre, Government of Canada. (2003). Online: **http://idl-bnc. idrc.ca/dspace/handle/123456789/26481**

These subsidies are used to pay the domestic farmers money in order to keep their prices artificially lower than they really should be in a free market. These tariffs and trade barriers are sometimes used against food producers in less developed countries, such as those in Africa, to reduce their ability to sell their produce and livestock competitively in the developed countries. If the subsidies given to farmers in the developed world were removed, it would mean that developing countries could rely on trade rather than aid to feed their people.

P. 148-149 In the U.K. 1/3 of food bought is thrown out as waste, a value of £10.2 billion per year.

Ventour, L. "The food we waste." (Banbury, Oxon: Waste & Resources Action Programme, 2008). Online: **http://www.wrap.org.uk/retail/case_stud-ies_research/report_the_food_we.html**

It is thought that most of this waste is avoidable and could have been eaten if only there was better planning, storage and food management. Less than one fifth is considered truly unavoidable food waste, such as bones, cores, and peelings. On a daily basis, 5 million potatoes, 7 million slices of bread, 4 million apples, and almost 3 million tomatoes are thrown away. Then another £1 billion is spent collecting this waste and transporting it to landfill.

P. 150 The transportation of U.K. food accounted for an estimated 30 billion vehicle kilometres (19 billion miles) in 2002.

Smith, A., et al. "The Validity of Food Miles as an Indicator of Sustainable Development: Final Report."

AEA Technology plc. Report for Department of the Environment, Food and Rural Affairs. (July 2005). Online: **https://statistics.defra.gov.uk/esg/reports/ foodmiles/final.pdf**

There are some emerging factors and trends that lie behind this statistic. Generally speaking, our food is being sourced from further away, even from other continents. Transport of food by air has the highest CO_2 emissions per tonne, and is happening on an increasing basis. Although air transport only accounts for 1% of the food tonne kilometres, it contributes 11% of the CO_2 food transport emissions. Then, rather than shopping locally, people are driving further to shop at supermarkets. In fact, the average distance for each trip has gone up by 50% in recent years. In order to stock the supermarkets, goods are routed through large out-of-the-way distribution facilities, resulting in even more food miles. All of these food transportation patterns contribute to CO_2 emissions, pollution, congestion, accidents and noise.

P. 151 A survey showed 50% of U.K. retail chicken is contaminated with Campylobacter.

"UK-wide Survey of Salmonella and Campylobacter Contamination of Fresh and Frozen Chicken on Retail Sale."

Food Standards Agency. (February 2003). Online: **http://cot.food.gov.uk/search?p=UK&srid=S22& lbc=food&ts=cot&pw=campylobacter&pu=1319& uid=775505203&mainresults=mt_mainresults_ yes&w=ukwide%20survey%20of%20 salmonella%20and&rk=2&sec=%2F**

Campoylobacter is a bacteria that causes food-poisoning. The cited survey highlighted the high incidence rate of this bacterial disease in the British chicken population. It is not possible to overstate the importance of ensuring that chicken is fully cooked, underscoring this is the fact that more than 40% of the Campylobacter strains found in chickens proved to be resistant to at least one antimicrobial.

P. I52-I53 The intensive raising of chickens is asso-ciated with many serious welfare concerns such as extremely high stocking densities, feed restriction, beak trimming and forced moulting.

Sahan, U., Ipek, A., and Dikmen, B.Y. "The welfare of egg layer, broiler and turkey." Faculty of Agriculture, Turkey. (2006). Online: **http://www.animalscience. com/uploads/additionalfiles/wpsaverona.htm**

These stocking densities mean that a chicken may be raised in a space no larger than a sheet of paper for its whole life. Pecking is a natural reaction to the overcrowding. The industry response to pecking is either beak trimming or de-beaking. Both are very painful procedures that involve cutting through bone, cartilage and tissue. Egg-laying hens are subjected to yet another painful experience. In order to unnaturally provoke a new egg-laying cycle, hens are made to endure a process known as forced moulting. They are kept in the dark, and starved for up to 14 days at a time. It is common for 5%-8% of the hens to die during this process alone.

P. I54-I55 American farmers' share of the average food dollar has dropped by 44% since 1982.

Stewart, H. "How Low Has the Farm Share of Retail Food Prices Really Fallen?" Economic Research Service, U.S. Department of Agriculture. ERR-24 (August 2006). Online: **http://www.ers.usda.gov/ Publications/ERR24/**

In 2004 farmers received 19% of the retail price for fresh vegetables. Back in 1982, the comparable share of the food dollar was 34%. In the intervening years an increasing number of middlemen have become part of the series of transactions that takes our food from farm to table. This change in the com-mercialisation of food means that farmers end up getting less, yet we are likely to be paying more since there is "value" being added along the way. We are now paying extra for food packaging, trimming and washing. It is worthwhile considering that by shop-ping at farmers' markets the biggest possible share of the food dollar is going directly back to the farmer who grew your food.

P. I56-I57 More than 335 million U.S. tons of manure are produced each year at animal feeding operations in the U.S.

"FY 2005 Annual Report – Manure and Byproduct Utilization." Agriculture Research Service, U.S. Department of Agriculture. (2006). Online**: http:// www.ars.usda.gov/research/programs/programs. htm?np_code=206&docid=13337**

This rate of production is 13 times greater than the rate at which human waste is produced. Some of this ordure is accumulated in large storage lagoons, pre-senting a significant pollution risk due to potential and actual leakage. The majority of the manure, however, is sprayed onto agricultural cropland in order to pro-vide soil and crop nutrients. Incidentally, these waste products also contain growth hormones, antibiotics, and pesticide residues from feed. Repeated spray ap-plications may end up concentrating the levels of these chemicals in the soil, and thereby crops.

P. I58-I59 Biosolids refer to sewage sludge that has been treated and then sold as fertiliser, often still containing pathogens and contaminants.

"Biosolids Applied to Land: Advancing Standards and Practices." National Research Council. (Washington, DC: National Academy Press, July 2002). Online: **http://www.epa.gov/waterscience/biosolids/nas/ complete.pdf**

Sewage sludge is the solid, semisolid, or liquid residue that is the end product of domestic sewage treat-ment. In order to avoid depositing it into the oceans or landfill, it is treated and then applied to agricultural land as a soil enhancer. The reality is that despite being treated it still contains a variety of undesirable chemicals and pathogens. These contaminants include heavy metals, infectious organisms, pharmaceutical residues and toxic PCBs. Although standards exist as to allowable levels, they are not monitored or reviewed on a regular basis. There have been anecdotal reports and lawsuits claiming illness as a result of proximity to soil treated with these biosolids. Finally, it is unknown what the cumulative effect is of repeated applica-tions of biosolids in the same area and whether these contaminants become concentrated.

P. I60 Scientific researchers are now convinced that red meat, along with processed meat, causes colorectal cancer.

"Food, Nutrition, Physical Activity, and the Prevention of Cancer: a Global Perspective." World Cancer Re-search Fund / American Institute for Cancer Research. (Washington, DC: AICR, 2007). Online: **http://www.aicr. org/site/PageServer?pagename=res_report_second**

The last decade has provided increasingly compelling research about this preventable cancer. Despite being a good source of nutrients like protein and iron, the irrefutable evidence is that red meat and processed meat need to be thought of as a potential health risk.

Limited evidence also exists linking these meats to other cancers such as lung, pancreas, oesophagus, endometrium, and prostate. Globally, we are seeing meat consumption rise due to increased income, and its status as a symbol of prosperity. As a result, before too long these health concerns will be felt around the world.

P. I6I Vitamin D is now being thought of as an effective means of protection against multiple sclerosis.

Niino, M., et al. "Therapeutic potential of vitamin D for multiple sclerosis." *Current Medicinal Chemistry*. 15.5 (2008): 499–505.

The lack of vitamin D used to be associated with bone diseases, such as rickets. This nutrient is now, however, taking on a protective role against many of the worst diseases we currently experience. For example, the incidence of multiple sclerosis is almost zero in the equatorial countries, where natural vitamin D from the sun is plentiful. Moving further away from the equator results in dramatic increases in MS. Abnormally low levels of vitamin D are now also seen in people with cancers such as colon, breast, prostate, and ovarian. Additionally, low levels of vitamin D seem to play a similar role in the occurrence of Parkinson's disease.

P. I62–I63 Stroke damage to the brain can be reduced by a diet high in spinach, blueberries and spirulina.

Wang, Y., et al. "Dietary supplementation with blueberries, spinach, or spirulina reduces ischemic brain damage." *Experimental Neurology*. 193.1 (2005): 75–84. Online: **http://www.cyanotech.com/pdfs/spirulina/sptl17.pdf**

A scientific study demonstrated that the extent of brain damage due to stroke was significantly reduced when a diet high in spinach, blueberries and spirulina was followed. Not only was there a reduction in stroke damage, there was also evidence of increased post-stroke mobility.

P. I64–I65 Coconut oil has been much slandered, yet communities which derive most of their fat calories from coconut oil are unfamiliar with heart disease.

Prior, I.A., et al. "Cholesterol, coconuts, and diet on Polynesian atolls: a natural experiment: the Pukapuka and Tokelau Island studies." *The American Journal of Clinical Nutrition*. 34 (1981): 1552–61. Online: **http://www.ajcn.org/cgi/reprint/34/8/1552**

Coconut oil has a neutral effect on blood cholesterol and, if anything, supports cardiovascular health. It contributes to weight loss because it is burned immediately as fuel, not stored as fat. Coconut oil is also known to increase the metabolism. Furthermore, it has antimicrobial properties. In essence, this means it's a natural antibacterial, antiviral and antifungal. This is particularly significant for those with gastrointestinal difficulties, candidiasis, and fungal infections.

P. I66–I67 Dark chocolate is not only very high in antioxidants, but it can also lower blood pressure and help with insulin sensitivity.

Grassi, D., et al. "Short-term administration of dark chocolate is followed by a significant increase in insulin sensitivity and a decrease in blood pressure in healthy persons." *The American Journal of Clinical Nutrition*. 81.3 (2005): 611–14. Online: **http://www.ajcn.org/cgi/reprint/81/3/611**

It's hard to believe that something so delicious can also provide all those health benefits. Yet, the antioxidant power of dark chocolate is on par with that of green tea. The potency is in the cocoa powder, so you can now consider a cup of hot cocoa a health drink.

P. I68–I69 In London alone 6.9 million tons of food is consumed in a given year, and 81% of it is imported from outside the U.K.

Best Foot Forward Ltd. "City Limits: A resource flow and ecological footprint analysis of Greater London." Chartered Institution of Wastes Management Environmental Body. (12 September 2002). Online: **http://www.citylimitslondon.com/download.htm**

The context of this report was to measure the ecological footprint of the city of London. Looking forward, the hope is to reduce this impact enough to achieve sustainability by 2050. Goals related to food consumption and transportation will require a shift to more locally sourced food, a reduction in meat consumption, and a reduction in household food wastage.

P. I70 A U.S. study showed carrots can travel 1,838 miles (2,958 km) to reach the plate, however if they're sourced locally they only travel 27 miles (43 km), almost 70 times less.

Pirog, R., and Benjamin, A. "Checking the food odometer: Comparing food miles for local versus conventional produce sales to Iowa institutions." (Ames, IO: Leopold Center for Sustainable Agriculture, July 2003). Online: **http://www.leopold.iastate.edu/pubs/staff/files/food_travel072103.pdf**

There is an increasing tendency for our food to travel greater and greater distances to reach us. It may be driving further or it may have taken a plane ride from another continent. The end result is that the salad on your plate may have travelled a staggering number of collective food miles, especially if it is out of season.

P. I7I High blood pressure, or hypertension, can be reduced by eating celery.

Ezzell, C. "Celery studies yield blood pressure boon." *Science News*. 141.19 (1992): 319. Online: **http://www.thefreelibrary.com/Celery+studies+yield+blood+pressure+boon-a012248197**

This appears to be old news in Chinese medicine circles, but is a relatively new approach in the Western world.

The active compound is apigenin, a flavonoid that acts by allowing the muscle walls of the blood vessels to relax, which makes them wider and allows blood to flow with reduced pressure. Anecdotally, eating about four stalks a day seems to provide noticeable improvements. Taking celery seed extract is another means of accomplishing this effect. Studies have also demonstrated that celery can lower cholesterol, as well as provide diuretic and anti-inflammatory benefits.

P. 172-173 Cranberry juice is effective in reducing or eliminating the incidence of urinary tract infections.

Stothers, L. "A randomized trial to evaluate effectiveness and cost effectiveness of naturopathic cranberry products as prophylaxis against urinary tract infection in women." *The Canadian Journal of Urology*. 9.3 (2002): 1558-62.

This is great news for those that experience recurring UTIs. Either drinking cranberry juice daily or supplementing with cranberry juice tablets will reduce the incidence of UTIs by half. Even better, 40% fewer women would experience UTIs at all. With their high antioxidant content and powerful anti-bacterial and antiseptic properties, cranberries have also been shown in various studies to have a significant impact against the incidence of cancer, most notably tumours of the prostrate.

P. 174-175 Garlic is a strong immune stimulator and can also inhibit the growth of cancer.

Shukla, Y., and Kalra, N. "Cancer chemoprevention with garlic and its constituents." *Cancer Letters*. 247.2 (2007):167–81.

Since ancient times, garlic has been reputed to have a number of health advantages, from warding off colds to helping with acne, and even controlling cholesterol. Its most dramatic effect, however, is its potent anticancer action. Garlic's inhibition of cancer growth is brought about by its direct toxic attack of cancer cells. Secondly, this pungent bulb can also neutralise carcinogens. Finally, it can even restrain the growth of transplanted cancer cells by stimulating the immune system.

P. 176-177 One out of every four children under five – or 146 million children – in the developing world is underweight for his or her age.

UNICEF. The State of The World's Children 2007. (New York, 2006).Online: **www.unicef.org/factoftheweek/index_39378.html**

Amongst the developing regions of the world, child malnutrition is most severely felt in South Asia and to a lesser degree in sub-Saharan Africa. For nutritionally deficient children, common childhood ailments such as diarrhoea and respiratory infections can often prove fatal. Even if severely malnourished children manage to survive their early childhood years they frequently have low levels of iodine, iron and protein. These deficiencies diminish energy levels, which in turn contribute to chronic sickness and a failure to thrive both in terms of physical and mental development.

ACKNOWLEDGEMENTS

First, an immense thanks goes to Christine Dirkschneider for her dedication in helping to create the photography. This would have never been possible without her support and vision. We would also like to thank Iris Feinberg in assisting with the book cover design, Adam Michael Feinberg, Derik Nelson, Marla Z. Munoz, Makenna Jean Dirkschneider, Jonathon Jonas, and Jeremy Ballard who posed for the book. In loving memory of Erin Gaston and Sydney Lynn Gross.